Signals from the Bible

Other Books by Harry M. Kuitert

The Reality of Faith
Do You Understand What You Read?

Signals from the Bible

by

Harry M. Kuitert

translated by Lewis B. Smedes

William B. Eerdmans Publishing Company
Grand Rapids, Michigan

Translated from the third Dutch edition (1967) of De Spelers en het
Spel, *published by W. Ten Have, N.V., Amsterdam, The Netherlands;
Copyright 1964 by W. Ten Have, N.V.*

Foreword

I want, first, to ask the reader not to demand more from this little book than it was meant to give. My intentions were rather modest, and I will be more than grateful if it can be used just for what I had in mind. What happens besides that is pure bonus.

My purpose is simple: to take several of the key words, phrases, and concepts of the Bible and let them offer us a chance to listen again to the Bible's own signals. Experience shows that even the person who is well versed in the Bible can close his ears to the signals it actually sends.

The educated reader will be able to spot the many books I have plundered, and how I have simplified some theological (and philological) studies. I hope he will be able to read my gratitude for the learned studies between the lines.

I have not tried for completeness. Many of the biblical concepts and words need to be restored to their original meaning and force. Anyone wanting to hear more will have to buy a large biblical lexicon or theological word study. Perhaps what is found here will be enough to make a beginning. I have tried, with the order I have used, to set the biblical language in a certain frame; the reader may notice how one thing leads to another, and all to the conclusion.

I have kept the contents from being topical or obviously relevant to the times. I want the readers to make the application for themselves, especially should any of them use the book in Bible study groups.

H.M.K.

Contents

1
Do You Understand What You Read?

Do you understand what you are reading? The question is as old as the Bible. We meet it in Acts 8:30, and here it provokes a question in return: How can I, unless someone points the way?

It all turned out well. So well, in fact, that the man went away a new person, rejoicing on his way. And we ask: Isn't this the whole purpose of the Bible?

To experience the purpose of the message, we shall have to understand what we read. This little book is meant to be a help—a sort of *mini*-guide, not to stand by itself, but to add a touch or two to other bigger and more important guides.

To learn the language of the Bible—this is what we are after.

First, the obvious question. Don't we now understand the Bible's language? It is written in plain English. Yes, but, as everyone knows, the English is translation. The writers used Hebrew and Greek. And to have it all in English, the whole thing had to be changed over, re-told. But even if it had been written in English from the first, we would still have trouble understanding the language. Anyone who reads the King James Version knows what a relief (or shock) it is to pick up a modern translation.

But in translation the question of how to understand the language gets harder. Translation is a difficult job; some people think it is impossible. It becomes harder as the translator is removed farther in time from the original writer. A personal letter from someone in Holland to a relative in the United States, let us say, is no big problem. The two people share much of the same history, the same religion, the same culture. So the two letters have much in common, even though the languages differ.

But take a letter from Tibet to a stranger in the U.S. Now translation is quite another task. Between the two people lies an enormous gulf: geographic, historical, religious, economic—everything. There is hardly a layer of cultural sameness. So the languages are likely to have very little in common, and translation gets harder.

Now take the Bible. There is really very little that old Israel and modern Europe have in common. Israel was actually a rather primitive people, living in a world—the ancient Mid-East—that no longer exists. This alone makes translation a brain-cracking adventure. Can we really grasp what these ancient writers *meant* to say? And can we really carry their meanings over from an ancient (dead) language into our very different modern tongues?

But this only opens the door to a room full of tough problems. Israel is not only a group of people who come to us from a time long gone, a culture long dead; they are the people of God, chosen from among many other ancient people to be God's elect. There they were—a little island in the sea of nations. Their special status makes translation of their writers even more difficult; it means that the Old Testament has its own special ways of expression, different even from those of the other ancient peoples. Israel was reared by God Himself—and for many centuries. "He has not dealt thus with any other nation" (Ps. 147:20); this is a factor that must be taken quite seriously. Only after Israel had muffed its chances did other peoples (*we* heathen, Rom. 11:11) have their day with Israel's God. The New Testament is full of amazement at the way God's salvation has turned out. "To the Gentiles also God has granted repentance unto life" (Acts 11:18).

But Gentiles are still Gentiles; they do not become Israelites even when they become attached to Israel's God. The question is: Will they understand what Israel's God meant when He spoke to Israel in Israel's words and in Israel's history? Will they understand it as Israel understood it? I suspect that "we heathen" will have to be a bit modest here (see Rom. 11:20). Our modesty will have to keep us from claiming instant understanding of what God intends with His creatures and this world.

What is written is written. No one can change the text. "We write you nothing but what you can read and understand" (II Cor. 1:13). Everyone can read it. But can everyone get hold of what the writers themselves understand by their words, their figures of speech, their own special idiom? To read the words on the page is one thing. But to grasp the inner sense, to hear the inner ring, to feel the inner meaning—that is another, and more important, thing.

A small example. In Psalm 119:25, the writer says: "My soul cleaves to the dust." A good parishioner told me that this obviously means that the writer's soul was too taken with earthly things. He exclaimed: "That's what the book *says*. Soul, cleave, dust—what better sense could we make of it?" But the authorized Dutch version adds this explanatory clause: "That is, I am as good as dead." The translators were sure that this and not the other is what the writer intended. And they were probably right. Notice the next line: "revive me according to thy word." The word "dust" points to something other than material goods, and the cleaving soul means something different from loving things too much.

But how does one know these things? Well, there is no quick answer. Anyway, this is the point of this little book. It is a modest offer of help in reading the Bible. Perhaps by digging some familiar examples of words, figures of speech, favorite expressions, and the like, out of well-understood passages, we can hear some signals. Only signals though!

Perhaps the reader will use them to begin some exploratory diggings for himself.

One more thing. We will be using the Old Testament often. The Old Testament was the whole Bible for the writers of the New Testament (see John 5:39; Luke 24:27). They were reared on it (II Tim. 3:15) and built their own writings on it. Whatever new things the New Testament writers had to say, they said them as much as they could in the language and images of the Old Testament. So if we want to understand the New Testament, we shall have to get well into the Old one.

2
God and the gods

The gods of the Bible pop in and out quite regularly. False gods, we learned to call them in Sunday School, but just plain gods in the Bible. They do not exist, we learned, and with that they lost their fascination for us.

But things are seldom as simple in the Bible as they are in Sunday School. How matter-of-factly some biblical writers talk about the gods (e.g., Judg. 11:24; I Sam. 26:17-19; Mic. 4:5)! They give us reason to suspect that we misunderstand them when we simply dismiss these gods as so much primitive foolishness.

To begin with, the First Commandment does not suggest that gods are simple nonsense and that to worship them is even simpler nonsense. The command says only that we are forbidden to worship the other gods (Exod. 20:3). This means: Israel's God demands for Himself the right to be Israel's *only* God. The others are competitors. But do the others so much as exist? It depends on what we mean by our word "exist." And here we enter a rather special path in the Bible.

Really, only Israel's God does exist—at least in the way the Bible understands "exist." For existence—or "being there"— means being there in a way that men can count on. "God exists," then, means: <u>God is God in a way that we can count on His being there for us.</u> This is why the Bible rings out every now and then with enthusiastic bursts like, "We also will serve the Lord, for he is our God" (Josh. 24:18), or "This is God our God" (Ps. 48:15), or "Who is like the Lord our God?" (Ps. 113:5).

But not everything that claims to be god can make good on the claim. All but one of them flunk out at the critical moment. That one exception is Jahweh, Israel's God. Many of the Psalms are written in the flush of this discovery. "For he spoke, and it came to be; he commanded, and it stood forth" (Ps. 33:9). And we can almost hear the afterthought—compare *this* with all the other gods! Or take another Psalm: "There is none like thee among the gods, O Lord" (Ps. 86:8; see also Exod. 18:11 and I Kings 8:23).

We find this sort of thing in the stories of the Old Testament too. Elijah's contest on Mount Carmel, for example, focused on the issue of which God was for real (I Kings 18). And, of course, the prophets are full of it, as for instance the magnificent passage beginning with Isaiah 44:6.

With this we hit on the most important mark of the gods, the mark that sets them off from the real God. They are *called* gods (or are treated as gods), but when it comes down to it, the name is a fraud. They cannot do what a god can be expected to do. They cannot give grace and they cannot execute judgment. "There was no voice; no one answered, no one heeded," says the reporter about the response the prophets of Baal received on Mount Carmel (I Kings 18:29). These gods? They don't do anything at all.

Jeremiah puts it hard when he calls the gods "scarecrows in a cucumber field." They are mere images. "Be not afraid of them, for they cannot do evil, neither is it in them to do good" (Jer. 10:5). This is why the Bible says over and over that there is no God besides Jahweh (Isa. 44:6; 45:5) or that the gods are not really gods at all (Jer. 2:11; 16:20). The writer of Deuteronomy puts them down as novice gods (Deut. 32:17). So it comes down to this: The gods do not act in a godly way, and this is why they are not really God.

But there they are, every now and then, putting on godly masks. The believing Israelite would not want to use the expression "there they are"—at least not in the authentic sense of the phrase. The Old Testament often calls them a "delusion" (Jer. 10:15) or "vanity" (Ps. 31:6), or sometimes "nothings," as the Hebrew language has it in such passages as Isaiah 2:8 and 41:21-24; and Psalms 96:5 and 97:7. We would call them phonies. The Bible writer wants to say with the word "nothing" or "nothingness" that even though someone *is*, he really is *not*—not genuinely—if he does not *do* what he ought to do.

The Old Testament uses such expressions for people too, or for the lying words of people (we shall speak of that later). But they fit the gods especially well. For they "have mouths, but do not speak; they have ears, but do not hear"—and so forth.

So God and the gods face each other in the Bible as the Real One who "can" and the others who "cannot." Poor people, those who left the Real One for the gods. The gods are never satisfied until they see blood (I Kings 18:28), and still they do nothing. As Israel learned first-hand, life is miserable when it is lived under the gods. But when the Bible preaches that the Lord is God, it amounts to this: God demonstrates His reality by doing what He should be expected to do. And this is why biblical preaching is tied to action. The fact that in the midst of all the gods and lords (I Cor. 8:5) there is one real God and one real Lord, means that there is only one under whose lordship life is good, only one who dares to look at blood, but would rather shed His own. Under the regime of the gods people become useless, too. But in the Kingdom of the real God people become real people. For the real God can be recognized in a crowd of thousands by one thing: He is for *man,* pro-people. Wherever we meet something or someone who is against people, we can be sure we have come across a mere god—even today.

3
God in His Acts

The Bible writers seldom use long adjectives to describe God. Some readers say that this is because the Bible writers were intellectually unsophisticated, or at least unsystematic. The suggestion lurking around the corner of such remarks is that we grasp things a bit more deeply today than the Bible writers did. But we really cannot read the Bible with this attitude. No matter how different the world is today from the world of the Bible, no matter how differently we have to talk today than the writers of the Bible talked, we can say biblical things *our* way only after we have understood them in *their* way, what they actually intended to say to us in *their* language. If we fail here, we are actually assuming control of the text rather than letting the text control us. We let the text control us only as we let ourselves listen to the Word of the Bible. Becoming a real listener—this is the first step to understanding. And, as we know, the real hearer is also the doer.

The Bible's so-called unsystematic way of talking about God has to do with something else. God is God *in the doing* of His wonderful acts. The Bible does not *explain*

God by listing the attributes of His deity (His eternity, infinity, omnipotence, etc.). The Bible does not explain God and then go on to say that this well-explained God also does things. Rather, God's qualities are revealed in the things He does.

This is why the Bible is mostly a book of stories. It starts with a story of what God did and ends with a promise of what He is going to do. The stories, one after the other, show God in action, liberating people here, judging them there, and letting it be known what He is like. Since God does these things and since He *reveals* Himself by doing these things, it follows that the Bible is going to be primarily a book of history. That is the Bible for you. It is not a primer on theology which learned theologians explain in huge volumes. It is the story of the God who shows the capabilities of His Godness by what He actually accomplishes.

"There is no God," for the Bible writers, would be about the same as saying, "He does nothing." If you ask, "But what sort of God is He?" the Bible writer is likely to reply saying, "Praise him for his mighty deeds" (Ps. 150:2). This sentence comes at the end of the Psalms, but the whole book of Psalms revolves around the mighty acts of God. "Give ear, O my people, to my teaching," says the Psalmist in Psalm 78. And what is the teaching? It is "the glorious deeds of the Lord, and his might, and the wonders which he has wrought" (vs. 4). And then follows the tale, epoch-style. This is the way the Bible gives lessons about God, the way the Bible teaches.

When you deal with a God who shows what He *is* by what He *does,* you have to explain Him by telling His story. And since He was Israel's God, telling God's story means telling Israel's story too. Many Psalms follow this pattern; some of them strike readers as strange ways of writing meditations, but they actually are just the way to write poems about the God of Action (see Pss. 97, 105, 106, 135, and 136). The Psalms, in this sense, are recitals, recitations of God's acts, and so of the revelation of His majesty. And for this reason they are cameos of the entire Old Testament, valuable clues to what the Old Testament is really all about.

But the Psalms are sometimes glum with complaint, too. They grump about the absence of God as well as praise Him for being about. When God forgets to be gracious (Ps. 77:9)—that is, forgets to be God—we will have to recall the other, better times: "I will call to mind the deeds of the Lord; yea, I will remember thy wonders of old" (Ps. 77:11). Still another facet is this: When God seems to have left us alone, we are driven to hope for the future, when Jahweh will undo what happened while He was gone. Then we will not bother to think about the past anymore (Isa. 43:18 ff.).

With this we arrive at the story of Jesus. For this story too is the account of God's mighty acts (the *magnalia Dei*). At Pentecost everyone heard the disciples proclaim the powerful acts of God (Acts 2:11). This, then, is what the church is for—to proclaim these things further (I Pet. 2:9).

One more thing about the mighty acts. Besides the call of Abraham, the liberation from Egypt, and the crusade in Canaan (the events to which the Old Testament mostly refers), we also have the story of the creation of the world. The creation is one of the stories where God demonstrates who He is—in action. The Bible writers tend to pick up the creation act and set it within their celebration of the other acts of God. You may have noticed this in, for example, Psalm 74:12-17, where creation is seen as God's victory over the chaos. Creation is an act of blessing; in Psalm 89:9-15 creation is one of the many good things God has done for His people, one of the demonstrations of His "steadfast love." This suggests that we, the readers of the Psalms, would do well to read Genesis 1 and 2 as the story of God's act of "steadfast love" instead of as a "scientific" or theoretical answer to the question of how the world was fabricated.

4
The Preface to God's Acts

We have not said enough even when we have said that God displays His deity in His great acts. It is not enough because it is still too vague. For the heathen too have their stories about what their gods do. We must ask: What is special about God's acts? Or we could put it this way: What kind of God do His acts reveal?

The answer brings us to a central motif in the biblical witness. It is almost fathomless in its implications. The answer is this: God shows Himself to be Israel's Covenant Partner. This is what is special about Him. This marks Him off. This exposes His essence, His peculiar character—or whatever word you can locate to show that God's being a Covenant Partner is the very essence of what we should confess and proclaim about God.

Almost every recent interpreter agrees that this is what the "I am who I am" of Exodus 3:14 is about. We should not read the cryptic words as a philosophical statement about the "eternal essence" of God—whatever that may be. It should be read as a sentence that God used to introduce Himself as the God who is a Covenant Partner, and who is about to demonstrate this in what He does. Let us pursue the text of Exodus 3 for a moment. God explains to Moses what He meant by the "I am." Moses is commanded to say to the people of Israel: "The Lord, the God of your fathers, the God of Abraham, the God of Isaac, and the God of Jacob, has sent me to you: This," says the Lord, "is my name for ever, and thus I am to be remembered throughout all generations" (vs. 15).

Whatever else we discover about God that is worth our praise, He apparently thinks it the greatest honor to be remembered as the God of the Covenant. It would be, I think, a mistake for us now to go into a study of what the word "covenant" means. We can save that for later. The word abounds with various contours, to say nothing of surprises. But we have gotten to the heart of "covenant" when we have said that God is the Covenant Partner.

God's great acts in Israel's life have a Preface. It is the story of Abraham. Abraham's story begins with a word spoken to him: "And I will make of you a great nation, and I will bless you, and make your name great, so that you will be a blessing" (Gen. 12:2; see also Gen. 13, 14, 15, and 17). In the same vein, a word comes beforehand at the moment of the great liberation from Egypt, when God revealed Himself definitively as Israel's God. God tells Moses that He has seen Israel's misery and is about to free the people from it and lead them into the land "flowing with milk and honey" (Exod. 3:7 ff.).

The Preface is powerfully recalled through the entire range of the Bible. It opens to us the Gospel of Matthew, for Matthew, uniquely among the evangelists, is concerned with the fact that the Christ is fulfilling and must fulfil the Scriptures (Matt. 1:22; 2:15, 17; etc.). As a typical Israelite, Matthew not only was tuned to God in action, but was shaped by the Preface. When he preached Jesus as *the* great liberating act of God in history, he used the whole Bible (what we call the Old Testament) as a Preface to his proclamation.

We should not stiffen the Preface by calling it things like "predictive prophecy." The Prefaces are more like promissory words by which Jahweh binds Himself to the fathers of Israel and, repeatedly, to Israel itself. This helps explain why the Prefaces are often referred to as the *oath* that Jahweh swore (e.g., Ps. 105:9 and Acts 2:30). God ties Himself to Israel so securely that He stakes His very Godness on it. He *is* this Covenant Partner and expects to be appealed to on that ground. Hence the call to the name of Jahweh that we hear throughout the Old Testament is an appeal to God as the Covenant Partner (see Pss. 25:11;

31:4). Sometimes the appeal borders on disrespect and presumption. But possibly the Old Testament writer knew how to pray more authentically than we do.

Herein lies the source of a lot of tension in Israel's experience: Is God being true to His bond? Is He sticking to what He began in His Preface? Sometimes the tension is very painful. "Where is He, why does He not do something?" ("O God, do not keep silence; do not hold thy peace or be still, O God"—Ps. 83:1). But then how delicious and full of hope are the words of Genesis 21:1: "The Lord visited Sarah as he had said, and the Lord did to Sarah as he had promised. And Sarah conceived, and bore Abraham a son in his old age at the time of which God had spoken to him." The Lord did as He said.

Who then is God? We cannot learn it from a textbook. But we can learn it from stories that tell us of His going in and out among His people with His words and deeds. God is a *He*, a *Someone*, who spoke His binding word—first to Abraham, then to Israel, and finally to us in His Son (Heb. 1:1). He is Covenant-Partner God. Not an It; not the "ultimate being" or some such nonsense. Not a "cause," not even the very first cause. Not a fate that someone may break his head against. Not nature, not even the power of nature with its horrible and lovely faces. These are all names for the gods. And as to gods, it is characteristic that they are silent at the crucial moment. That is, they leave lonely people adrift in a speechless universe.

Israel's God does not keep silent. He speaks the words that bind Him to His people, and then does things to bring the words to life. This is how He defines His being; this is how He interprets Himself. Let me make a big leap. John uses the word "interpret" when he proclaims what Jesus came to do. Jesus is the *Word*, the Word from beforehand, before all things that would occur (John 1:1). "No one has ever seen God; the only Son, who is in the bosom of the Father, he has made him known" (John 1:18). He has *interpreted* God for us. He who has seen Jesus has seen

God at work, interpreting Himself as our Covenant Partner (John 14:9). Nonetheless, the appearance of Jesus Christ (the Word) is, in its turn, a Preface. We still wait for the fulfilment.

With this, the enormous role of the little Bible word "faith" is involved. Believing means to invest our existence in this Preface and so wait for the hour when God finishes His deeds. Believing, thus, is living, living between yesterday and tomorrow.

5
The Partnership

The Bible is not limited to stories in its message of the God who binds Himself in a covenant with Israel, binds Himself with words and in deeds. It has its own word for this bond, a word that shows up regularly in both of the Testaments. It is "covenant," or "partnership." What did the Bible writers think of as they wrote this word?

To begin with, we could try to get the feeling of what a partnership in ordinary human affairs means to Bible writers. The most obvious aspect seems to be that all covenants have the same purpose. Partnerships are aimed at bringing two people into a peaceful relationship. The basic assumption of a covenant is that peaceful association is an elemental necessity for human life. Life is life together in peace on this earth.

In a few cases, social life is carried on in a way that makes peace seem like a natural style of life. In these cases, a covenant is hardly needed. Family life is probably the clearest example. Brothers illustrate to the psalmist how

peaceful associations are formed without special covenants
(Ps. 133:1).

A covenant is needed only when peaceful life together
does not just happen by nature. When two people from
families that are enemies swear to be partners (David and
Jonathan, I Sam. 20:12-17) we have a covenant. Or when
the heads of two families make an agreement (Jacob and
Laban, Gen. 31:44 ff.). Also, when two peoples (or their
kings) decide to stop war and live in peace (Solomon and
Hiram, I Kings 5:12). In short, a covenant in whatever
situation has but one purpose: to establish human association in peaceful ways. Even cosmic peace—between men
and nature—is put in the context of a covenant by Hosea
(2:17) and Ezekiel (34:25)—a covenant God intends to
establish between men and animals. A covenant makes
brothers out of strangers. This is why it is called a Jahweh-
covenant in I Samuel 20:8. Jahweh will see to it that the
new bond of brotherhood between David and Jonathan is
never broken.

It is important to note that a covenant does not require
equal partners. Often one partner is weak and only too
eager to accept an inferior role if it brings him some peace.
Consider the case in I Samuel 11, or Joshua 9:6, or I Kings
20:34. It is still a covenant relationship, for it secures and
supports a peaceful association, no matter how tenuous
the peace may seem to be. The particular form in which
the covenant is molded often depends on the comparative
capabilities of the partners. A covenant does have to do
with reciprocity (and thus with free decision). Without this
there could be no covenant. But a covenant does not
require reciprocity between partners of the same standing.

When the Bible is stressing the inequality of man and
God in their covenantal relationship, the overpowering
superiority of the great Partner, then the word "covenant"
hovers over the territory of another important biblical
word—"election." We can recall here all the times that
Jahweh reminds Israel that the relation between them was

begun at His initiative. Genesis 17, certainly, says this in all clarity (see verse 2, in which the Hebrew language says: "I shall give my covenant"—evidently the expression "my covenant" says enough).

The New Testament continues to sound this accent. Here the Greek word for covenant sounds like a kind of final disposition—and in some cases it is translated as "testament" (e.g., Gal. 3:15 ff.). This obviously stresses God's decision. But other writers use the word "covenant" precisely to underscore the significance of the *human* partner, what the lesser party is supposed to *do* as covenant partner. And in this context, covenant stands on the same level with commands (Deut. 4:13 ff.). To keep the covenant is to obey the commands (Exod. 19:5; Josh. 7:11, etc.).

But both accents are needed to express the basic point of the covenant: "I will be the God of all the families of Israel, and they shall be my people" (Jer. 31:1). What is the relation between God and man about? It is about trust, love, peace—reciprocally between the two partners. True religion is living as God's covenant partner. And knowing who this God is, we must quickly add that to live as His partner also means living as the covenant partner of man.

The covenant partnership is an ongoing relationship in which the whole content of Scripture is dramatized. This is why the main line of the Bible is so intensely interesting. In the covenant we have a freely willed reciprocity, and because it is this, we are really *concerned.* How will it end? How are the partners getting on? In a freely willed partnership tomorrow can never be taken for granted. This is why the New Testament comes by way of *promise* (Jer. 31:31 and Luke 22:20).

And so, too, if we talk about one of the partners we cannot help talking about the other—just because we have to talk about them *as* partners. We can never talk about God by Himself, and we cannot talk about man by himself. We have to talk about both of them if we talk about either of them. If we do not, we are not talking about the real God (the Covenant Partner of man) or the real man (the covenant partner of God).

6
Shalom

Peace is the heart of the covenant. This is why the words "covenant" and "peace" are so often found in tandem (e.g., "covenant of peace," Ezek. 34:25; 37:26). Sometimes they are exchanged for each other (I Kings 5:12 and Ps. 55:20, 21). Once the covenant is sealed, the partners go in peace (Gen. 26:28-31).

Biblical usage suggests that the Hebrew word *shalom* carries more freight than does our word "peace." *Shalom* connotes such things as prosperity, abundance, growth, fullness. One friend could ask of another: "How is it with your *shalom*?" (Gen. 29:6). He is asking about the other person's general well-being. David, for example, asks about Joab's *shalom*. He also asks about the *shalom* of the war (II Sam. 11:7). Now to ask how the *peace* of the war is getting along is utter nonsense. But to ask about the *shalom* of the war does make good sense because it means to ask about its success. In another area, Zechariah 8:12 asks about the *shalom* of the seed. And in Psalm 38:3 the poet says: "There is no *shalom* in my flesh." Its parallel, in the same verse, says: "There is no health in my bones."

When a person has *shalom*, then, he has health, blessedness, well-being. So, when we come across the familiar passages that speak of peace, we ought not shrink the word down to "peace of soul" alone. *Shalom* describes a very concrete, tangible situation, at least in the main lines of biblical thought. The mountains that "bear *shalom*" (Ps. 72:3) are the mountains where corn grows well (Ps. 72:16).

Wherever the poet prays for the "*shalom* of Jerusalem," he is asking for the city's prosperity in the full sense of the word. He is praying for its total well-being. He has his eyes on such things as Psalm 72 sings about and as Psalm 85:9-14 pictures. The last passage is very interesting. The poet says that Jahweh shall talk about *shalom* (vs. 8). *Shalom* is where a genuine fellowship is created. But Jahweh *is* Israel's Covenant Partner, and thus Jahweh *is Shalom.* Gideon had also understood this (Judg. 6:24). To stick with Jahweh is to know well-being, growth, and prosperity.

No wonder, then, that the major prophets seize on *shalom* as *the* magnificent perspective for the future. When the judgment is passed, Jahweh will give *shalom* again (e.g., Jer. 29:11; Isa. 54:10, 13; 57:19). Again, this is a *shalom* that is as earthly as life and health. For instance, Isaiah pictures *shalom* as a condition in which wild beasts no longer frighten people—a picture that is a favorite for the prophetic artists (Isa. 65:25; 11:6-9; Ezek. 34:25). It is also Isaiah who especially associates *shalom* with the Prince of Peace (9:5, 7). *Shalom* shall prevail without end under His regime.

All in all, *shalom* is a condition of things on earth. It is a lot more than the mere absence of hostilities, though this is part of it. It is a blossoming of life, an enjoyment of God's world, an unbroken fellowship of God and man that is hardly imaginable in our world today. This explains why wounds are the opposite of *shalom* (Jer. 8:12; 14:17; see also the parallel between healing and peace in Isa. 53:5). The picture of wounds suggests that a break has taken place in the peace (because of the infidelity of Israel to its partnership; partnership and peace go together). It is a breaking up that destroys *shalom.*

But what does the New Testament say of *shalom?* In the

main it stays in the tracks of the Old. The coming of the Messiah, the Prince of Peace, brings out the angels, who sing: "*Shalom* on earth" (Luke 2:14). The true king of *shalom* (Heb. 7:2), the genuine Solomon (kingdom of peace) has arrived. Now the prophecies of *shalom* have come full to earth. The Gospel of *Shalom* (Eph. 2:17; 6:15; Acts 10:36) is proclaimed to the world. The *shalom* condition involves peace with God—and with men. Of course! We have already noticed how inseparable the covenant partnership and *shalom* are. This explains why, in one place at least, the word "peace" means precisely "peace *with* God." But this is an exception. In most places *shalom* peace is a state of affairs that God creates; He is the God of peace (Rom. 15:33; 16:20; II Cor. 13:11; etc.). He creates a life without breaks, a life on earth that is whole.

Because Jesus has come, *shalom* has already begun. "He *is* our peace," says Paul in the present tense in Ephesians 2:14. In Him we *have shalom* (John 14:27; 16:33). But the New Testament also preaches Jesus as the One who is still to come. And in that sense we are still looking ahead for peace, along with all our brother Christians (Heb. 12:14).

Only when *shalom* is "all and in all" will God have had His way. And only then can we be satisfied.

7

The Earthly

The Bible is full of the Gospel *for* this earth. But this earthly direction of the Bible's message is a stumbling block for many. It somehow seems out of place to put so heavy a stress on this life, on this earth.

Many people are a little ashamed to admit their interest in earthly things. Heaven seems so much more proper for Christians to be concerned about, and is probably more of what the Gospel is about. Perhaps these people will have a hard bout with this chapter.

But if the Bible is as concerned with this earth as it indeed is, has not something gone afoul with our reading glasses if we don't recognize it? The earth is not denigrated by the Bible. "The heavens are the Lord's, but the earth he has given to the sons of men" (Ps. 115:16). The earth is our true element, as the water is for fish. It is given by Jahweh, but it is His gift for men. We shall have to work hard to find anything denigrating about the earth in this fact. The Psalmist is not likely to sing: "This world is not my home." Heaven and earth are not competitors for our affection.

Men on earth can become competitors of God in heaven; and in that sense this earth can be the *scene* of competition. But we are never asked to choose between heaven and earth. The Bible writers are earthly, and with a good conscience. And they did not come to this on their own. God Himself is very earth-inclined. His acts are for the good of this earth. And His good intentions are directed not only toward the inner man—He is out to do good to the whole man. His acts of mercy are not only spiritual, they are so concrete we can reach out and touch them.

We see this in the way the Old Testament talks about God's blessings. It is all a very tangible matter (Job 42:12 ff.; Joel 2:14; Mal. 3:10). The promises He made to the fathers and later to Israel are hardly spiritual in the sense that spiritual is other than earthly. When the covenanting word is said, the promise of a large family goes with it (Gen. 12:2; 13:16; 15:5 ff.). And large families are earthly things.

And once Israel has become a people to be reckoned with, it is constantly reminded of "the *land* I shall give you"

(Exod. 20:12, and especially Deut. 12:9 and 25:19). A land of milk and honey no less. Anyone wondering how Israel understood this promise ought to read Deuteronomy 8:7-9. The land promised here is ordinary, real, earthly land. Once the land is occupied, Jahweh Himself comes to promise the Israelites a "long life"—which in the Bible is a sign of a blessed existence (see Zech. 8:4, 5)—as long as they follow His way (Exod. 20:12; Deut. 11:9; see too Eph. 6:3). He also promises rest from their enemies around them (Deut. 12:10; 25:19) so that every man can live safely under his own fig tree (I Kings 4:25).

The entire movement of salvation history, with its attendant acts of God, aims at the time when Israel need buy no acre of the land, but will have it all as an inheritance. The reader should consult, for example, Genesis 33:19, Exodus 32:13, and Deuteronomy 1:18. We find the same perspective in the prophets as they scan the future in their preaching. The picture Isaiah paints of the "new earth" is a picture of *this* place, created by God (Isa. 65:17 ff.). There is hardly a passage in the prophets that does not gaze upon the same scene. The prophets are concerned with real men living on a real earth. Or to put it in larger focus, they are possessed with a vision of the covenant partnership with God that God's men have in their history on this earth.

The earth is not merely the showcase or theatre of God's great acts, as Calvin has called it. The acts of God are *for* the earth, for men in their relations with God and each other, relations that are tied to life on earth. Genesis 2:7 says that Jahweh formed man out of the dust of the earth: *dust-man* is his real name. The Bible writers would be confounded if their message of peace were read as anything but peace on earth. Isaiah (65:17) and John (Rev. 21:1) climax their prophetic message with the assurance that God will indeed finish His program with the creation of a new heaven and a new earth. The success of redemption does not entail the disappearance of the earth, but rather that the meek shall inherit it (Matt. 5:5).

But then, we may ask, what of heaven? What of those Pauline expressions telling us that we are to be liberated from the earth. Such expressions remind us that when we have said what we have said in this chapter, we are not finished. We shall have to ask what the Bible tells us about heaven too.

8
Heaven

If it is true that the earth is in the foreground of the biblical picture, it is not true that heaven lies in the background. This must be insisted on, even though heaven does not play the same role in the Bible that it does in a lot of Gospel hymns.

Let us have a try at drawing a few broad strokes around the Bible's way of looking at heaven.

(1) First, heaven refers to firmament, in the technical sense. A large umbrella (Gen. 1:8) covers the earth like a tent (Isa. 40:22). It is, to the Israelite's eye, something like a huge tarpaulin that divides the waters above from the waters beneath the heaven (Gen. 1:8; Ps. 148:4-6). The earth appears to be a large flat pancake surrounded by water. It is not only lying on water (Pss. 24:2; 136:6)—with the coastlands being the "ends of the earth" (Isa. 42:4)—but is covered by water above the earth, behind the heavens, or firmament. (Psalm 104:3, in keeping with this, says that God "laid the beams" of His own living quarters on the waters.) So much water—a fearsome thought! The Israelite responded this way too, especially when he recalled the great flood, and was reassured only as he remembered that God held the sluices both above and below

the earth (Gen. 7:11). God's faithfulness consisted in this: that He kept the water within its boundaries and did not let it flood the earth again (Gen. 9:11; Job 38:8-11; Ps. 104:9; Prov. 8:29).

(2) God lives up above. Heaven is His established living place, according to a common biblical way of speaking (Deut. 26:15; I Kings 8:30; Isa. 63:15). He speaks to men from up in heaven; He hears, sees, and carries on battles from heaven. Heaven is Jahweh's palace (Ps. 104:3), complete with throne (Dan. 7:9; I Kings 22:19). Now the writers mean by this to say something not about cosmic geography, but about the ways of God. His "heavenly throne" is a manner of pointing to His majesty and power. He who lives in heaven can laugh at the "kings of the earth" (Ps. 2:2-4). We should think of His throne in heaven as a way of saying that He really does rule, that He really is king (Pss. 11:4; 103:19). The writers even like to underscore the power of God as creator by saying that He established His throne in heaven; now, therefore, "the world is established; it shall never be moved" (Ps. 93:1). To be creator is to have a throne in heaven. This is what thrones in heaven are all about (in addition to Ps. 93, see Ps. 95:3-5 and Pss. 96-99).

(3) Heaven is not only the royal residence. It is also the curtain behind which God hides Himself, sometimes to the point of exasperation (Isa. 64:1; see also Job 22:12 ff. and Lam. 3:44). Wherever we read about Jahweh's throne in heaven, we are made aware of an element of hiddenness (I Tim. 1:17 and 16:15 ff.). Not least, the hiddenness and mystery of His acts!

We must also think about the ascension of Jesus at this point. For the ascension means not only that Jesus is elevated to the throne of God, but also that He is hidden behind the curtain of heaven (Col. 3:3) until He comes again (Acts 3:20-21 and I Thess. 1:10).

(4) Heaven is not only a veil behind which God conceals Himself; it is also a curtain behind which is prepared

everything that God plans to give to men. The tabernacle was first planned in heaven before it was built on the plains of Sinai (Exod. 25:9, 40). The manna came from heaven (Exod. 16:4). All of God's supplies are there, His reservoir of good gifts for His own. So James can sensibly tell us that all good gifts are from above (James 1:17). The whole Bible speaks this language. Heaven is the place where God's treasures are ready, stored safely for the great day. Neither moth nor rust can hurt them (Matt. 6:19-21). Heaven is thus the place that the Messiah came from ("the bread from heaven"—John 6:32). We expect Him to come again from there, along with all His blessings (I Thess. 1:10; II Thess. 1:7).

In brief, we may say that one day everything will be heavenly. Not, of course, that the earth is to be lifted up to heaven. Just the other way around. Heaven will come to earth, and everything here will be quite heavenly. It was all begun for the sake of the earth, and that goal has never been shifted, neither in the Old Testament nor the New. Indeed, heaven must come to earth before the earth can really come into its own as God's earth: a new Jerusalem "coming down out of heaven" (Rev. 21:2).

(5) But are we not going to heaven when we die? Thank God, the Bible talks only sparingly of this. In Philippians 1:23 Paul does of course speak of our going to heaven when we die (though John 14:1-3 is not really telling us this). But heaven provides in this instance a sort of temporary residence. Heaven is a waiting room. Happily, the Lord is there (II Cor. 5:8), but it is still a waiting room (Rev. 6:9-11). Our final reward is earth, the Kingdom of God that shall come *here* (Matt. 6:10).

True, the earth has been badly spoiled by us, and so Paul tells us to "put to death . . . what is earthly" in us and seek the things that are above (Col. 3:1), namely, Christ and His will. It is also true that one day we will bear the image of the *heavenly* man, Jesus Christ—heavenly as opposed to what is earthly (I Cor. 15:47-49). But all this

does not imply that we are to say good-by to the earth; it
means rather that we must say No to the *un-earthly*
earth—the earth that is corrupted and no longer what God
made it to be. "When Christ who is our life appears, then
you also will appear with him in glory" (Col. 3:4). This is
the last word—and the ultimate intention: that we shall
one day be able to say that the earth is truly heavenly.

9
The Image of God

Before we go on to talk about what life in partnership
with God is like, maybe we had better take one more look
at the human partner. In the creation story, man is called
the image of God. "So God created man in his own image,
in the image of God he created him; male and female he
created them" (Gen. 1:27). What does the writer of Genesis mean?

Image here seems to be something like an ordinary
copy, in the literal sense. We find the same notion in I
Samuel 6:5, where people were instructed to make images
of the tumors and mice with which the land was ravaged;
the people were meant to make little reproductions in
brass. The word likeness is a bit less specific. But it too is
used in the sense of a model. In II Kings 16:10-12, Ahaz is
reported to have constructed a model (likeness) of a heathen altar that he had seen in Damascus.

Genesis 1:27 seems to be telling us this: Man is a model
of God; in some ways he resembles God. (The word
"likeness" keeps things a bit loose here.) God's Godness is
the model for man's manness. With this, the writer wants

to tell us (preach to us) what man's humanity actually is. Created on the same day as the animals (man's fellow creatures), related to the earth (the dust out of which he is made), he is nevertheless distinguished from all other creatures (even though he too stays a creature). He is distinguished because only he has God as his model. To be a man is to look like God.

But this does not complete the story. Being an image entails a special purpose. To get at this purpose, we can best recall something about the religious images of the ancient world. With these images, too, we have the notion of looking like something. The more closely an image resembled the god it represented, the more powerful the image was, the more it could do for you. The resemblance was what made an image effective. An image or idol of a god served as the visible representative of that god among the people. And this helps us understand why Jahweh wanted nothing of idols of Himself among His people. His reason was not that He is immaterial. (It had more to do with the idol's impinging on His freedom; Israel could not and ought not to try to coerce God's presence among the people by having Him represented in the idol.) But it had everything to do with the fact that God already had an image on earth, man. And though Genesis 1 proceeds from the thought that being God's image involved something like being a representative of the original, Genesis 1:28 reminds us that the man who looks like God is the man who rules over creation. He is manager of God's affairs on earth. To look like God is man's glory (Ps. 8).

This is wonderful, but we must also ask how things are going with God's image today. Even after the fall, we find Genesis 5 stressing man's likeness to God. And Genesis 9:6 returns to it (and I Cor. 11:7 and James 3:9). These passages hardly suggest that man has altogether lost the image. On the other hand, we discover the New Testament telling us that man has to be *renewed* to the image of God his creator (Col. 3:10; Eph. 4:24). The apostle Paul seems to say that the image has been lost. How do we bring these things together?

We can get farthest if we consider that the Bible writer thinks of man's looking like God primarily in terms of man's concrete actions. Man (and, for that matter, God) is always seen as the concrete, living, acting person, a being who exists in his doing things. (Man as sinner is the person who *acts* sinfully—Col. 3:9.) When man is called a copy of God, we must not imagine a still-life portrait or a snapshot. We must imagine him doing things in the way God does them. To be a man is to reflect the way God does things, to reflect this in our own doing of specific things.

Do we really mirror God? I mean, do we really reflect the God of the Bible? The God who comes to us first of all as Covenant Partner? Are we a covenant-partner kind of creature, toward other men as well as toward God? This is the question!

To look like God, to be His image, is not something we can do simply by being rational creatures or by having a good will. We cannot see God in man while man stands still. To look like God has to do with the purpose God has for man. The question, then, is what is man for, what is his calling? What is he here for? He is here to reflect God, to reflect God the Covenant Partner. To be God's image means simply that we as men are to live as covenant partners with God and with our fellows on earth.

The fact that man is called to be a covenant partner in action belongs to the very essence of what it means to be man. This is why the Gospel can be summed up as the restoration of man to God's image. Paul thought this way in Ephesians 4:24 and Colossians 3:10. It is for this reason that he speaks of Jesus as *the* image of God (Col. 1:15); that is, Jesus in His life of action is as like God as one drop of water is like another. When Jesus' acts, we cannot separate His acts from God's acts. And this is what Jesus said: "He who has seen me [in action] has seen the

Father" (John 14:9). "I and the Father are one" (John 10:30).

To this thought Paul can attach the further one that we are re-created after the image of the Son (Rom. 8:29). But this means that we are reshaped in a way that allows us to mirror the Father too (II Cor. 3:18). And we had better begin with the job today (Rom. 12:2).

To look like God, then, involves a summons to follow God. Like loving children we are to imitate God (Eph. 5:1). Here is the destiny of man; here is the purpose of having humanity. This too is part of the Father-son relationship. To be a son (a child) of the Father ought to end in the son's looking like the Father—in the right sense, of course (Matt. 5:44, 45).

10
The Character
of the Covenant Partner

We have finally come to ask what life in the covenant is like. Till now we have talked of some important foundation realities: God reveals His Godness in His actions, and man in his turn becomes a real man in terms of his life's actions. We have also seen that these actions (including the spoken word) are God- and man-revealing acts if they are the acts (and words) of covenant partners. Also, the man who is a covenant partner is man-on-earth, and the peace that he knows through his covenant partnership is a peace on earth, even though its origin is heaven. Now the way is clear to consider what sorts of actions covenant-partnership actions are.

What does the genuine covenant partner do? The Bible

uses some key words to describe his behavior pattern. It often applies these words to God's actions as well as to man's. We shall fasten on four of these words, taking them in pairs. Together they add up to a sketch of the covenant-partner life.

Righteousness and Justice

We in modern times tend to think of righteousness as giving to every person what he has a right to have. The Bible means this much by the word, but it means more. Righteousness is the quality that makes a covenant partner authentic; by carrying on in certain ways a man demonstrates that he lives as a partner—and this is not quite the same as merely giving every man his due. Righteousness is, therefore, a defining quality of the covenant partner.

Righteousness is very often mentioned in the same breath with justice (II Sam. 8:15; I Kings 10:9; Isa. 9:6). When we think of justice we think immediately of the court and of the judgments of rulers. The Bible writers had the same idea. The king, who is the highest judge in Israel (II Sam. 15:2), is the one who must execute justice (I Kings 10:9; Jer. 22:15). But the ordinary man must do justly as well. When we read about the "ordinances" (in Exod. 21:1, for example), the intention is clear. The covenant partners abide by certain laws which spell out the right ways for covenant partners to act. Justice, then, is the concrete covenant-like action that is expected of the righteous man. (These actions are of course going to have a different style in the case of kings than in the case of common people.) Whenever anyone lives up to these expectations, he demonstrates his righteousness and does justly.

Goodness and Truth

The combination of "goodness and truth" is found in the Bible as often as that of "righteousness and justice" (about thirty times in the Old Testament). The two words are often translated as "steadfast love and faithfulness" (e.g., Pss. 25:10 and 89:14—RSV). Let's begin with the second word in the coupling, "truth."

The Bible writers do not have precisely the same notion of truth as most of us do. The word gets its meaning from the covenant partnership and is used to describe partnership kinds of actions. Just as righteousness is what one must do as a covenant partner, truth is what one must be and do in the midst of things that happen, in the shifting scenes of time and history. This is why the Bible writers speak of God's covenant actions as true as well as righteous (sometimes as both, e.g., Zech. 8:8). Truth is that which makes one trustworthy in the face of the unknown future; to be truthful is to show faithfulness.

Goodness—or loving-kindness—is to truth what justice is to righteousness. It is the *exercise* that is demanded by the truth, as justice is the doing of what is demanded by righteousness. Truth is disclosed in concrete acts of loving-kindness (acts of faithfulness or loyalty). All in all, the words are understandable only in the living relations of the covenant partnership, the relationship between God and man and between man and man (consult Deut. 7:9 to see how the words we have been talking about are intertwined with the word "covenant").

The words "righteousness" and "truth" both help to define an authentic covenant partner, and for this reason they too, like "righteousness and justice" and "goodness and truth," often come in tandem (I Sam. 26:23; Zech. 8:8). Similarly, both "justice" and "goodness" point to what gives character to the concrete acts in which righteousness and truth take shape.

If we wish a New Testament example, John 1:14 will do. Christ is described as "full of grace and truth." Or, as I John says, He is "faithful and just," which is what the Old Testament would call truthful and righteous. The New Testament too gives us passages which are understandable

only as we read them from the perspective of the grand
purpose of revelation—the covenant partnership (e.g.,
Rom. 3:1-8).

11
Righteousness (I)

Looking at the situations in which the word "righteousness" appears in the Bible, we notice one thing right off:
the writers of the Bible pack more content into the word
than we usually do. Luther ran up against this fact when
he first grappled with Paul's praise in the book of Romans
for God's righteousness. Praise? Must we not tremble in
fear before the divine righteousness?

We would normally react as did the young Luther. The
word "righteousness" sounds threatening to us; we hear
severity and punishment in it. But if we look at Romans
1:16 and 17 we do not hear this at all. Here "the righteousness of God" is the power of God to preserve us and
protect us. God's righteousness offers the sinner protec-
tion; it does not threaten him with destruction. How is this
possible? To understand this, we have to follow the paths
that the Bible blazes with the word "righteousness" and its
derivatives. Under what circumstances might the Israelite
talk about someone's righteousness?

We can begin with a couple of pertinent examples.
Curiously, an Israelite spoke of *things* as being righteous.
There were "righteous ways" (Ps. 23:3) or a "righteous
scale" (Lev. 19:36). A "righteous" way is a way that
brings one to where he wants to go and a "righteous" scale
is one that works accurately. In both instances the word
"righteous" points to a thing that functions properly,

meets its purpose; a thing is justified, therefore, if it does what one may expect it to do.

We can, without much fear of going wrong, work with this as the basic meaning of "righteous," whether it applies to God or to man. The judgments of Amos (or of Isa. 1) give us a typical picture of a breakdown of righteousness (which takes concrete shape in the doing of injustice). In other words, the Israelites failed to do what Israelites were expected to do in their concrete relationships. They were not in fact what they were meant to be—covenant partners with their neighbors. What they did do was oppress their poor and powerless neighbors (see Amos 2:6 ff.), and in doing so demonstrate the contradiction of righteousness. Job, on the other hand, can protest that he had never oppressed the "little ones" and therewith seek to prove his righteousness (Job 29:12-14).

That the poor and the weak are almost always mentioned is not accidental. It shows again, and clearly, that righteousness is more than the equal distribution of things for all. To see to equality is not yet acting as a covenant partner is expected to act. The weak need more than this, more support, more help than does one who is able to help himself. Righteousness is a many-sided thing, and acting righteously is a many-sided activity. Righteousness is one's faithfulness as a covenant partner (see Job's protestations of his own righteousness, and similar testimonies in the Psalms—e.g., Pss. 7:8 and 18:21, 24), and faithfulness to a partnership life can be demonstrated in every possible way that life's situations can offer. Nonetheless, in the Bible the first and most obvious way is to help the needy. We recall here Daniel 4:27, where "righteousness" means just about the same thing as "social action" or "benevolence." Matthew 6:1-2 makes the same identification.

The contents of the word "righteousness" do not change when the Bible speaks of God's righteousness. A very familiar example is Psalm 98, so familiar that its power is often overlooked. The King James Version reads: "The Lord hath made known his salvation: his righteousness hath he openly shewed in the sight of the heathen." What does this really say? The righteousness God has displayed is, if we notice, the revelation of His salvation. Time and time again the Psalms confront us with the fact that salvation is the content of God's righteousness. (This, incidentally, makes the parallels, the verses that say the same thing as a previous verse only in other words, very helpful in our effort to understand the Bible's language.) Consider, for example, Psalms 40:10; 88:12; 97:6; and 103:6. Isaiah, too, constantly identifies God's righteousness with the manifestation of His saving acts on behalf of Israel and the nations (e.g., Isa. 42:6; 45:8; 51:5).

To round this thought off: God's great acts of redemption, which the Israelites told to one another, are called God's "righteousness" or God's "just deeds." All in all, righteousness is the demonstration of covenant faithfulness. Righteous acts are acts which clearly stamp the doer as the authentic, tried-and-true covenant partner.

How much this helps us understand St. Paul's vocabulary of the "righteousness of God" and of "justification" and "the justified" remains to be seen in the next chapter.

12

Righteousness (II)

The apostle Paul uses such words as "righteous" and "justified" more than does any other New Testament writer. The question here is whether what we have seen in the Old Testament will help us understand Paul's usage. I think it will.

We must recall that Paul is in daily dialogue with the Jews of his day. The questions these Jews asked were the same ones that the Israelites of the Old Testament asked. They were all about the righteousness of God and of men. An Israelite was a real Israelite only as he was a real covenant partner; and he was a real covenant partner only as he had "righteousness" or, in other words, was "justified."

Nowhere does Paul dispute this idea. Why should he? Obviously, the whole business turned on one's being righteous, on what made one a genuine covenant partner. What Paul does deny is the notion that one's *own* righteousness makes him a righteous or just man (Phil. 3:4-11). In this, Paul has the Old Testament itself on his side, as he never tired of telling his Jewish opponents. The just shall live by *faith* (Hab. 2:4 is cited in Rom. 1:17 and Gal. 3:11)! What Paul means by this we must go on to see. In any case, he uses words like "righteousness" and "justification" in the same vein that we discovered in the Old Testament—to describe the true Israelite, the real covenant partner.

We can dig the contents of the word "justify" out of the Old Testament. We have to be alert to the Israelite way of pronouncing judgment, as this was done first by the elders at the gate (Job 29 and Ruth 4:1) and later by the kings of Israel (II Sam. 15:1-6 and Ps. 72). Israel had no prosecuting attorneys. Both adversaries simply came to the elders of the community who would then decide which of the two was in the right. That is, they decided which of the two had acted as an authentic covenant partner. The right one was said to be "justified" or was "declared just." The one in the wrong was "declared guilty." A neat example of this sort of judgment can be found in Deuteronomy 25:1-3.

Now, there is also an ultimate judge, God Himself. In the last analysis, things rest with Him: Shall He declare a man just or guilty? (I Kings 8:31, 32).

We can bring this way of talking into line with St. Paul's

vocabulary quite easily. When Paul talks about God "who justifies the ungodly" (Rom. 4:5) he leaves us no problem with what he means by "justifies." He means that a person is declared to be a true covenant partner. We must, of course, think here of a partnership not only between men, but between God and men as well. The true partner is he who combines obedience to the first and second commandment, who loves both God and his neighbor (Matt. 22:34-40).

"To be justified" must be understood as being established as a just person in the judgment of God, which is to say being established as an authentic covenant partner. God justifies; man is justified.

We can now be a bit clearer on why Paul constantly ties justification, which renders a person just, with faith—that is, why he speaks of the "righteousness of faith" (Rom. 4:13) or of being "justified by faith" (Rom. 3:28, 30; 5:1; Gal. 2:16; 3:24; etc.). Paul is contesting the notion the Jews (and even some Christians) had that a man came to be judged righteous (or just) by proving his own justness, by proving that he "possessed" righteousness.

Such "justification by works" (Rom. 3:20) was brushed aside as fiction. How could Paul be so sure of himself? If it were otherwise, Jesus could just as well have not come. The fact that Jesus did come was proof enough that neither Jew nor Gentile was able to stand before God as righteous (this is what Rom. 1:18-3:20 is about). It also demonstrated that God Himself had provided a better way for men to be righteous (this is what Rom. 3:21 ff. is about). The better way is what Paul calls the "righteousness of faith," the opposite of "righteousness by works." "By faith" means the same as "without works" (Rom. 3:28). But, now, why does Paul say that this righteousness is "by faith"?

Paul uses this expression to say that the new righteousness is really Jesus' righteousness. He is the real covenant partner; He is the just person who has taken the whole task of our humanity on His shoulders and carried it through to the end, to the happy ending. He was "raised for our justification," as Paul puts it so triumphantly in Romans 4:25. In a word, He equals us. This is the content of Christian preaching; on this everything stands or falls.

And this is precisely why everything also depends on faith, on the faith that puts its arms around this message. That is, a man of faith takes the equation "He equals We" with complete seriousness and therefore—with a sigh of complete relief—knows that he is accepted by God. Now, then, the phrase "justified by faith" means that Christ's righteousness is actually our own. This is the whole point. The "righteousness of faith" means the same thing. It is the righteousness of Jesus that makes us what we are, covenant partners of God.

Inasmuch as God Himself gave Jesus to us (Rom. 3:25; Phil. 3:9), Paul can also call the new righteousness the "righteousness of God" (Rom. 3:21 ff.). With this, he is saying no more than he said when he spoke of the "righteousness of faith." For he is saying only that this righteousness is a gift of God, a present (Rom. 3:24). This is also what the righteousness which is reckoned to us is all about (Rom. 4:4). With this, too, Paul is underlining the fact that we are not "justified by works" but by faith, and that this really means by Jesus Christ, which means by nothing that we do, which means by grace (Rom. 4:16)!

All of Paul's linguistic talent is played out in order to make this clear.

13
Justice

We are still working with the expression "justice and righteousness." The latter of these two words we looked at in the previous chapters. There we saw that the Bible calls a man righteous when he demonstrates himself to be a genuine covenant partner. But what then does a person have to do to prove that he is a reliable covenant partner? The answer is this: he must perform justice. Righteousness shows what it is in the doing of justice. This is why the two words are so often used together (Gen. 18:19; II Sam. 8:15; I Kings 10:9).

To do justice is to perform just *acts*. And the just act *par excellence* is to keep the covenant, to move it along, or, if need be, to restore it. This is the way, finally, to bring *shalom* on earth. For if there is going to be any peace on earth, it will have to come through the doing of "righteousness and justice" (Isa. 32:16 ff.)

But how can the just act be spotted for what it is, an act that keeps the covenant relationship going? Actual life points the way for us here. When we speak of "justice," we must think of a judgment, the like of which we often find in the Bible. To do justly is first of all to secure justice for the covenant partner (i.e., the neighbor) who is not "getting his rights," as we say. Everyone must do this if he is to perform his role as a covenant partner in human relations. But the job belongs particularly to the judges, to the elders at the gate and, ultimately, to the king. Whenever two people find themselves in controversy, they appeal to the judges and perhaps eventually to the king, who must judge between them, who must pronounce judgment (Exod. 18:16 ff.).

At this point, we make a surprising discovery. What sort of thing does the Bible make out the act of judging to be (think, for example, of the "last judgment"). "To judge"

means first of all to *secure* justice for the oppressed who
have not come into their rights. Psalm 72:1-4 provides a
nice example when it describes the job of the king in these
terms: "May he defend the cause of the poor of the
people, give deliverance to the needy." This is a com-
mentary on verse 2, which says that he shall "judge thy
people with righteousness." To judge means to come into
the controversy swiftly to insure the poor their rights (for
the "poor" we may also read the humble, the oppressed,
the miserable). We could also refer to the poor widow (the
symbol of the poor throughout the Bible) in Luke 18:1-8,
the woman who came begging for someone to secure
justice for her.

This brief examination makes it clear why the Bible
makes so much of God's judgment, of His securing justice,
and of the fact that people can appeal to His coming to
judge the earth.

In the most basic sense, to judge means to speed to the
help of the oppressed. When God rises to "execute judgment," He comes, as Psalm 76:9 has it, "to save all the
oppressed of the earth." Judgment, then, involves the
judge in securing the rights of the downtrodden (Ps.
103:6).

It is striking that the Bible constantly thinks of the
judge as someone people can *appeal* to when wronged,
especially in the case of God the Judge. God is the Vindi-
cator. For this is what it comes to most often. When
people appeal to God the Judge, they call Him to vindicate
their cause. And He comes to set the oppressed free (Pss.
9:4; 35:23, 24; 74:21, 22; 75:8; etc.).

Of course, vindication has its reverse side. Punishment
of the oppressor may not be the prime purpose of the
judgment, but it is very tightly tied to it. We see it in Psalm
72:4, where we read that God will "crush the oppressor."
This needs to be done. If the sheep are to get the room
they need, the wolves will have to be set at bay. If the
poor are to get their needs supplied, their oppressors will

have to be bridled. This is how the king demonstrates his justice in Israel. In the covenant life, all the covenant people are called to a "kingly" task. But it is still basically the king's job.

To be a king is to be a judge, is to be a liberator. Now if we set Matthew 5:1-12 (the Beatitudes) and Matthew 25:31-46 ("as you did it to one of the least of these my brethren") alongside the Old Testament notion of God the Judge, we will grasp what sort of proclamation Matthew is giving us about Jesus Christ.

But the word "justice" comes out in still another sphere. We have talked about the judge's officially executing justice. We now see that the word is used in reference to ordinary human behavior. In the Bible, a just act is one that sustains the covenant partnership, and obedience to covenant rules makes for just behavior. Hence the covenant rules are sometimes translated as "judgments"—though frequently also as "ordinances" (Exod. 15:25-26; 21:1 ff.). The point is that these are rules the covenant partner is expected to live by. The Ten Commandments are covenant laws. They outline a style of life that a person who is a covenant partner accepts as a matter of course. Not to live this way is scandalous "folly in Israel" (Gen. 34:7; Judg. 20:6). Ignoring the rules is "not done in Israel" (II Sam. 13:12).

In the broadest sense, just behavior becomes a matter of custom or usage; not all the laws are written. And if we include the general pattern of life in the covenant community along with the written judgments we get a picture of the just life—obedience to written or unwritten obligations that embody the covenant pattern of life.

14
Truth

Let's go back a step. The genuine covenant partner is not only the person who does "justice and righteousness," but also, as we saw earlier, the person who shows "mercy and truthfulness."

Once again, the Psalms are full of these expressions: "His mercy is everlasting; and his truth endureth to all generations" (Ps. 100:5—King James). We shall talk about His mercy in the next chapter. But now the word "truth." What are the Bible writers thinking of when they write "truth"? Do they think what we usually think?

Not exclusively. The Bible tips us off when it speaks of "*doing* the truth." This is not our style. But it is the warp and woof of the Bible, including the New Testament (John 3:21; I John 1:6).

Truth is, first of all, characteristic of the *actions* of a covenant partner—his acts of fidelity to the covenant. We have to be able to rely on a covenant partner. He has to promise something and then *do* it. He is not a man who awakens expectations in us and then lets us down. He is reliable. And when he does, his *actions* are truth.

This is why we are constantly being told that people have to demonstrate truth to their neighbors (sometimes the word is translated "trustworthiness"). That is, they have to show by their deeds that they are faithful to their covenant partnership (Gen. 47:29; Josh. 2:14; Judg. 9:19; etc.).

It applies as well to God. We hear that He demonstrates "truth" in His actions; that is, He shows that He is faithful to His covenant partnership (see Gen. 24:27). God's truth means the fidelity He demonstrates in His actions toward Israel. This is the truth that Israel praises in the sanctuary (Pss. 111:7; 117:2; 146:6). In this last text (Ps. 146:6—King James) the word "truth" is almost identical

45

with the word "covenant"; He shall preserve His covenant forever. Notice how the same thought comes out in Psalm 138:2, Psalm 40:12, and Isaiah 38:18 ff., where men appeal to His truth, that is, to the way He demonstrates His truth in His actions.

We can let it go at this; we have seen enough to examine now some typical ways in which the Bible speaks about "truth."

The Old Testament talks, for example, about a *"way* of truth" (Gen. 24:48). The "way of truth" is a way that does not let us down, a way that does not lead us into a dead end. So too, the red cord of Joshua 2:12 is a "sign of truth" (or "truth-symbol"). The intention is just about the same: it is a sign that you can trust, that you can act on.

God's commandments are also called "truth" (Ps. 19:9). His laws do not lie: we can confidently direct our lives by them without anxiety that they might mislead us. Take a well-known line from Psalm 25: "All the paths of the Lord are mercy and truth" (King James). These "paths" are not the paths on which God walks, but the paths that His commands blaze through life for us (see vss. 4 and 5). Of these ways, the writer says, they are *truth*—they don't lead us into a no man's land, but into familiar pastures.

We get closest to modern usage when we find the Bible talking of "speaking the truth." But here too a slight difference is evident, a difference that is associated with what we have just been noticing. For instance, in Genesis 42:16, Joseph demands certain actions of his brothers "that your words may be proved, whether there be any truth in you." This is what the search for truth is all about. As a man's actions can be tested to see whether he is an authentic covenant partner, so too can his words. The question was, Did Joseph's brothers deal with him in a trustworthy way, or did they deceive him? Could he rely on them, act on them? This is what the word "truth" is about. It has to do with whether people are *acting in truth* when they use *words.* Do we have clear signs that we can trust ourselves to them, or are they pulling the wool over our eyes?

The use of the word "truth" in the Old Testament is background for its use in the New. For example, in John 1:14, the eternal Word appears "full of grace and truth." This is a translation of "mercy and truth." God's mercy and truth, which so fill the Old Testament, are definitively revealed in Jesus Christ. Not that the Old Testament flavor is always this noticeable, for the word "truth" is used in the New Testament in many different connections, too many to mention all of them. But wherever it appears, it is of a piece with what we have already noticed: truth involves trustworthiness.

When "God's truth" is involved (e.g., Rom. 1:25), it has to do with the actions of God in which He shows His fidelity. When truth in general is meant (e.g., Gal. 5:7 and II Thess. 2:12) or merely "words of truth" (as in Eph. 1:13 and Col. 1:5), it has to do with the story of God's revelation in Jesus Christ—with the "Gospel," as Colossians 1:5 specifies. The Gospel is not called the "truth" merely because it contains words about God that are accurate, but because it is trustworthy without limit. It never misleads—and therefore must be obeyed (Gal. 5:7).

"Truth" is a key term in John's Gospel (like "light" and "life"). And John too rings the changes on trustworthiness with it. When Jesus says of Himself "I am the truth" (John 14:6), He means just what He says. It is not simply that He speaks the truth (though He does that); nor that He proclaims truths. He *is* the truth; as the One who reveals God to us, He is trustworthiness itself. For God is trustworthiness itself.

15
Showing Kindness

By "showing kindness and truth," God keeps His covenant moving through time. We talked of truth in the last chapter; let us move on to kindness, or mercy.

To be constant in one's covenant partnership—over the long haul this can be done only one way, by being consistent in word and deed yesterday, today, and forever. The Bible calls this consistency *being* the truth. And now we see that kindness is manifest when covenant constancy is demonstrated in the concrete actions of the covenant partner. The basic thrust of the word "kindness," then, is *fidelity* to another.

An example from a moment in Israel's life: David sent an ambassador to Hanun, king of the Ammonites, with the thought, as the King James Version renders it, "I will show kindness to Hanun" (II Sam. 10:1 ff.). Some translations have "friendship" for kindness. Now David had had a good working relationship with Hanun's father and was eager to continue the friendship with Hanun. So the gist of the "kindness" David wanted to show was this: "I am going to give a concrete demonstration of my wish to be loyal to our covenant relationship." The Revised Standard Version makes the point clear: "I will deal *loyally* with Hanun." (For the shabby return David got on his investment, see II Sam. 10:4, 5.)

Another example: Absalom meets Hushai coming to join the rebellion against David. Absalom knew well that Hushai had been a favorite of David and had been trusted by the king. So he asked Hushai, "Is this your kindness to your friend?" (II Sam. 16:16—King James). Here too the word "kindness" refers to covenant loyalty. Absalom was really asking: "Is this the way you show your loyalty to David?" (RSV: "Is this your loyalty to your friend?").

Kindness within the covenant comes down to covenant loyalty.

The word "kindness" is a core word in the Old Testament vocabulary, and these passages suggest why. The covenant between Israel and God was kept alive by mutual faithfulness and thus was a matter of constantly repeated acts of kindness. "I remember thee, the kindness of thy youth," says God to Israel (Jer. 2:2—King James). What the text means is this: "I miss the affectionate demonstrations of covenant loyalty that you once so faithfully gave me." The Lord is complaining, and the word "kindness" carries the weight of "loyalty" again (the RSV translates "devotion"). Hosea 6:4 suggests a similar complaint. Recall the lament, "O Judah, what shall I do unto thee? for your goodness is as a morning cloud" (King James). The word "goodness" here is the same as that translated "kindness." And what God is lamenting is the fact that Israel's covenant response, far from faithful, is as fickle as a morning cloud in Palestine.

A failure of covenant loyalty was par for the course in Israel's history. But for Israel's God, it was always the other way around. His loyalty is the theme of many songs, perhaps the most impressive being Psalm 136. Twenty-six times the refrain repeats it: God's kindness endures forever (see also, e.g., Pss. 107; 118; and 138:8). Seldom could it be said of Israel; always of God: He is forever the same (Heb. 13:8). The word "kindness" is so closely tied up with the covenant that here and there it becomes almost synonymous with it. For example, Deuteronomy 7:12 promises that Jahweh will "keep unto thee the covenant and kindness which he sware unto thy fathers." He would keep them, that is, *if* the people kept listening.

In view of all this, we cannot help wondering how it happened that Israel perverted the whole covenant reality into a work-righteousness—or self-righteousness, as Paul branded it. Israel misunderstood the entire covenant and radically distorted it. Of course, the covenant did call for reciprocity—this is clear enough. Even a covenant between God and Israel needed reciprocity! But this does not mean that reciprocity created and defined the covenant. Israel did not establish the covenant. Nor did Israel sustain it by reciprocal acts. This, in fact, is where the great mistake was made, a mistake that erupted with catastrophic results in Israel's encounter with Jesus Christ. The Jews supposed that their own obedience to the covenant law actually formed the basis of the covenant. This is why they were blind as moles to Jesus Christ, the personal embodiment of God's grace.

Now a word about "kindness" in the New Testament. The Greek translation of the (Hebrew) Old Testament most often translates the word "kindness" as "grace" when it comes to showing God's covenant fidelity, though it sometimes uses the word "mercy" (in John 1:14 we find "grace" and in Luke 1:72 we find "mercy" for the same word). This suggests very strongly that we ought to understand God's covenant faithfulness, in the Old Testament as well as the New, as something deeper than mere consistency with His verbal promises. The fact that the covenant was kept intact is owed to God's consistent readiness to *demonstrate* His faithfulness by concrete *acts* of "kindness"—or, if you will, His grace. And this involves somewhat more than remembering verbal promises.

When it is referring to the faithfulness of men to God, the New Testament uses the word "faith." II Thessalonians 3:2 uses the word "faith" for what is otherwise called "faithfulness." And thus "faith" in the New Testament is pretty much what was meant by "faithfulness" in the Old Testament.

16
The Controversy

The covenant life could go wrong; this was always a live possibility. It happened whenever "justice and righteousness" or "kindness and truth" were not evident in the life of the Israelites. When it did happen, "peace" was destroyed, or "the covenant broken." The word "break" suggests the opposite of "peace." *Shalom* (peace) means a life without gaps, without breaks. A break in the covenant life comes about when it develops cracks, when it loses its wholeness, when it gets chaotic. Another word for "break" is "hurt," or "wound." Jeremiah, for example, laments the "wound of my people" or the "wound of the daughter of my people" (Jer. 6:14; 8:11, 21; see also Isa. 30:26). The break is not necessarily a rupture of the covenant, but it is a breaking up of the *shalom,* or peace, of the covenant life.

To grasp the religious language of the Old Testament, we have to keep the situation between men and fellowmen clearly before us. Two partners can have a disagreement or controversy. Recall the story of Abram and Lot, and their controversy over the grazing lands. This particular kind of controversy is a matter of one party in a covenant being wronged. The man who is not getting his rights, or the man who, given the covenant relationship, feels he is being disadvantaged by the other party, has a controversy with that party. Thus David has a controversy with Saul (I Sam. 24:16) and with Nabal (I Sam. 25:39), with David praising God for avenging "the insult I received at the hand of Nabal."

The word becomes terribly important when we consider the covenant between God and Israel. Can we speak of a controversy, a suit, between these partners?

Consider the complaint that Israel raises against God in the desert. The name of the place—Meribah—is borrowed from the controversy (Exod. 17:7). But the writer leaves

51

no doubt that Israel's claim of being wronged by God was without basis in fact. Israel's controversy with God, its great Partner, is branded a tempting of the Lord (vs. 7).

Whether Jeremiah's complaint against Jahweh is legitimate is less clear (Jer. 12). May Jeremiah properly register a complaint against God, or may he not? We don't get a clear answer.

But the Scriptures make it clear that the complaint Jahweh initiates against Israel is entirely valid. Jahweh sees Himself dealt with unjustly by Israel, given their covenant compact. He has a controversy against Israel for its unfaithfulness. We encounter this constantly in the Old Testament (see, e.g., Hos. 4:1; Jer. 25:31; and especially the dramatic instance in Mic. 6:1 ff.). Happily, the Old Testament repeats this comforting word: He will not always chide. That is, He will not always quarrel (Ps. 103:9; Isa. 57:16). He's not that kind of God.

But we have not finished. Israel's God would not be who He is if He did not take up the controversy on behalf of the disadvantaged of the earth. One testimony which recurs throughout the Old Testament is that Jahweh takes on Himself the controversy, the complaint, of the poor, the oppressed, the disadvantaged among the people. The controversy David had with Saul and Nabal, God took up as though they were His own controversies (I Sam. 24, 25). He takes the matter into His own hands and carries the case to a happy ending. The controversy is part of a crucial drama in history, the drama of God's choosing the side of the oppressed party.

Jahweh's redemptive labors for Israel become His controversy with Israel's enemies. "I will contend with those who contend with you, and I will save your children," says Jahweh in Isaiah 49:25. That is, He promises to save His people out of the grasp of their enemies by making Israel's cause His own (see also Isa. 51:22).

This decision on God's part explains the appeal people make to Him: "Contend, O Lord, with those who contend with me" (Ps. 35:1). Or as Psalm 74:22 has it, "Arise, O God, plead *thy* cause." Israel's cause is Jahweh's cause. Herein lies the strength of the "servant of the Lord." Though Jahweh's servant is the oppressed and humiliated one, indeed the embodiment of all oppression, he yet triumphs because Jahweh takes up his cause and makes it His own (Isa. 50:6-9). Further, we see the quiet expectation that Jahweh is one day going to take the cause of His people decisively into His own hands (Mic. 7:9).

Having said this, it is hardly necessary to discuss the New Testament in detail. What is the history of Jesus Christ but the story of how God has taken into His hands the cause of His servant—and with it our cause—and made it His own (Acts 3:26; 4:27-30)?

Summarizing, then, Jahweh is the God who constantly takes up the cudgels for Israel, who makes Israel's cause His own cause. It was not that Israel was expected to do battle for Jahweh. That would have turned things on their head.

17
The Lord Repents

Recognizing the peculiarities of the language of the Bible involves us Western readers in some mental gymnastics. Sometimes the problem is created not so much by our ordinary Western language as by our dogmatic concepts. Theological vocabulary is not always the language of biblical writers. But often the problem is both our ordinary Western language and our theological jargon. Both are probably factors in our problem of understanding how God could repent of something He did or said. The Bible confuses us with its talk of the Lord's repentance. Does being God foreclose on the possibility of His repenting, or not?

The Bible strongly suggests that it does not. In fact, there is hardly an expression in the Bible that more clearly reveals what God is like than the expression "God repent-ed." By using this expression, the Bible writers underscore not only the living relationship between God and man, but the fact that God remains Himself and wants to remain Himself within this relationship. That is, He wants to keep on being the Covenant-Partner God.

Let's begin with the most familiar passage: "I repent that I have made Saul king" (I Sam. 15:11). There is nothing—outside of theological prejudice—to prevent us from taking these words seriously. Jahweh chose Saul to be king of Israel, but He felt hurt that He had to go back on His decision when Saul acted the part of an unfaithful king.

Repentance is not a matter of arbitrariness or fickleness on Jahweh's part. On the contrary, it is a consequence of His insistence on being true to Himself. While Saul fouled the lines of covenant partnership, Jahweh kept them straight. This is why He repented of having made Saul king. God can go back on His previous acts; this is what we are told. He can undo the situation, though it hurts Him, deep in His heart.

This turning in God (undoing a *good* intention as a reaction to Israel's unfaithfulness) crops up frequently in the Bible. The words that open the flood story are well known: "And the Lord was sorry that he had made man on the earth, and it grieved him to his heart" (Gen. 6:5). Enough to make a man want to bury his face in the ground! Notice how closely "repent," or being "sorry," is tied to "grief" in God's heart.

More often, however, God repents of the evil that He intended to do, and does not do it. In fact, we could say that the entire Old Testament appeals to the readiness of

God to repent. It is characteristic of God, as we notice in
Exodus 32:14 and Joel 2:13. The entire book of Jonah is
devoted to this divine characteristic, and though the word
itself does not appear, the same thought is found in such
passages as Exodus 34:6, Psalm 86:14-16, Psalm 103:7-11,
and Numbers 14:18.

It must be that God can act contrary to His first
intention and that this change is characteristic of Him.
(Another example is II Kings 20!) This is not whim. It is
God's covenant faithfulness. This is what it is all about.

Why did He not do what He announced He was going to
do? Why did He not destroy Nineveh? The answer is this:
He is merciful and gracious and full of loving-kindness.
And what was on Jonah's mind, with his dogma of God's
unchanging nature? He wanted to press God into unkind-
ness. He did not want God to repent. And this means that
he did not want God to be God. Jahweh is the God of
covenant relationships. He changes in the midst of the
concrete life situations of the covenant and in changing
proves that He is unchangeably faithful to His covenant.

But what of those expressions that tell us that God does
"not repent" because He "is not a man" (I Sam. 15:29;
Jer. 4:28; etc.)? They tell us the same thing. They underscore the drama that is being played off between God and
Israel. Not to repent means, I am utterly serious about our
covenant. Jahweh is not a fickle man; when His partners
contribute nothing but unfaithfulness, He rejects them.
Yet He can turn back even on this decision: "For thus says
the Lord of hosts: 'As I purposed to do evil to you, when
your fathers provoked me to wrath, and I did not re-
lent . . . so again have I proposed in these days to do good
to Jerusalem and to the house of Judah; fear not' " (Zech.
8:14, 15). The last word is that "the gifts and the call of
God are irrevocable" (Rom. 11:29; King James, "without
repentance"). But, one may say, this is the very epitome of
inconstancy: back and forth, in and out. Two things must
be said in reply. What does God reveal in this "in and out"

process but that He is the same covenant-faithful God to the uttermost? He is faithful with us in *our* in-again, out-again lives. Then too, do we not rest in the hope that He can find it in His great heart to repent His "unrepentance," and let His "last" word be followed by His *final* word—the word of Grace?

18
A Jealous God

Let us stay awhile in the area of God's repentance. Another characteristic of the Lord that indicates His emotional involvement with us and points to His covenant faithfulness is jealousy. As with "repentance," our understanding of the word "jealousy" is hampered by our theological concepts. Sometimes dogma prevents us from understanding what we read.

We associate jealousy with smallness of spirit and we resist the notion that God could be so petty as to be jealous of anything or anyone. But what does the Bible mean when it says that God is jealous? What sort of language is it using? The Bible writers have to teach us how to talk about God. What do they mean, then, when they call God a jealous God?

The ordinary—as distinguished from the specifically religious—language of people can point the way. Numbers tells us in what sort of situation the word is most at home—the marriage covenant. If the marriage vow is broken by the woman, the man has every right to be jealous. To be jealous really means to be intolerant of a rival.

Numbers 5 suggests that the society of that time was a male-dominated society, patriarchal in its structure. The

woman was always the one who could not sin against the
marriage vow (and this is still the case in many Eastern
lands). We hear practically nothing of the man who is
involved (see, e.g., John 8:1-11). It is the husband, then,
who is jealous. Now Jahweh's jealousy has to be seen in
this light, for the covenant between Him and Israel is a
kind of marriage covenant (e.g., Exod. 20:5; Deut. 4:24;
Jer. 2-4; Hos. 1-3; Ezek. 16). The prophets mean to show
the intimacy that exists between God and His people. But
they also—and especially—want to stress the exclusive
rights Jahweh, the husband of Israel, has to His bride. The
rights of the husband belong to Him alone: He possesses
the people. He is honorable, and His honor is Israel. And
Israel's glory is God (Jer. 2:11). Jahweh brooks no rival;
the more real the marriage, the less He permits His bride
the luxury of an affair with another. Put it this way: We
can measure the faithfulness of His covenant by the inten-
sity of His jealousy. Were He a less passionate husband, His
jealousy would not be so keen. The Bible speaks of God's
wrath in the same manner. Here too we can make the
equation that His wrath is measured by His love. If God
did not love so strongly, He would not become so angry.

In this atmosphere, the word "jealous" is a beautiful
word. It belongs to the language of love. Only a suitor can
be jealous. Hence the expression "to provoke to jealousy."
It is precisely because God is a loving husband that Israel
can move Him to jealousy. Israel stirs up jealousy when it
whores after other gods (Deut. 32:16, 21; I Kings 14:22;
Ps. 78:58; Ezek. 8:3).

All in all, one thing is clear: God's jealousy is a far cry
from pettiness. Jealousy can, of course, take this small-
minded form. One can covet something that belongs to
another (Job 5:2). People are like that. But this is because
they are poor examples of covenant partners to each other.
Israel's God is the authentic Covenant Partner. He does
everything on behalf of His partner, everything to His
partner's advantage, everything to make things turn out

well for him. The Greek gods present a striking contrast here. They were jealous of their wards' prosperity; when their protégé prospered, they called their relationship off. This sort of divine jealousy is only a projection of human jealousy. It has no similarity to the jealousy of Israel's God.

One more thing needs to be said. Sometimes instead of "jealousy" we find the word "zeal." This happens where the emotions of love alone are involved, where no rival is in the picture. People may have zeal for the Lord and for His house. Elijah, for example, says, "I have been very jealous for the Lord, the God of hosts" (I Kings 19:10). Paul admits that the Jews had a "zeal for God" (Rom. 10:2). And the Psalmist cries, "For zeal for thy house has condemned me" (Ps. 69:9). But God's great zeal for Israel is even more intense. The misery of Zion burns within Him. And so redemption will come: the *zeal* of the Lord of hosts shall see to it (Isa. 9:7; 26:11).

19
Redemption Is Liberation

The Hebrew word that is often translated as "salvation" or "redemption" really means *liberation,* as any good lexicon will remind us. The family of words that it stems from has to do with "space"—as in "to give someone room." What the Israelites understood by redemption is to be freed from cramped quarters and put into wide spaces.

There is a special expression in the Old Testament that provides an exact picture of what we just said: "He brought me forth into a broad place" (II Sam. 22:20). And this same thought is repeated many times (Pss. 18:19; 31:8;

118:5). The reality of redemption has to be thought of in this way, that is, to be liberated from confinement and set free within broad spaces. When Jonah felt cramped in the belly of the whale, he did not talk of salvation or redemption, as many translations have it, but of freedom from his cramped confinement, from his claustrophobia (Jon. 2:9).

It is remarkable that most translations generally turn the word "liberation" into "salvation." When Psalm 88:1 sings of the "God of my salvation," for example, it might better be given as the "God of my liberation." For this is what the Psalmist is talking about. Liberation sums up everything God was doing and would do with the Israelite. The words "liberation" and "liberating" are truly at home in the language of the Israelite writer.

The book of Judges, for example, is a continuous story of liberation, of freedom from confinement (Judg. 2:15, 16; 3:9, 31; 6:14, 36; etc.). Israel's experience, typically, is that she wanders away and falls into the hands of an enemy, and that God then comes to liberate her.

The history of Israel is a story of liberation, beginning with the Exodus from Egypt. (The Passover was always an independence day celebration.) From the Exodus on, its experience is one liberation after another. When Isaiah exults in God's overcoming of Egypt and the others, he sings it out: Israel's God is a liberator (Isa. 45:15).

The Psalms could be called Songs of Liberation. Not that all of them sing of deliverance; there are complaints and confessions too. But a large number are indeed hallelujahs to God, to God who creates breathing space and leads His people into it, to the God of liberation. The Hebrew word for liberation appears no less than sixty times in the Psalms. Jahweh's deeds are great acts of freedom (Ps. 74:12 ff.). In Psalm 32:7, the Psalmist exults: "Thou shalt compass me about with songs of liberation." Another instance of such praise is Psalm 107. Isaiah 45:15 also sings of God as liberator, or deliverer. A liberator is a figure with more tough manliness than some of our children's Bible stories like to portray. But this is what He is in the Old Testament—the great Liberator.

Sometimes the liberating judges of the Old Testament, the men sent by God to free His people in distress, are called saviors (Othniel and Ehud, for instance). And the name of the coming Messiah, who will liberate His people for good, is Savior too (Isa. 19:20).

From here we can turn to the New Testament. The name of the Messiah, says the angel to Mary, is to be Jesus, "for he will save his people from their sins" (Matt. 1:21). This translation explains why the Heidelberg Catechism (Lord's Day 11) says that the name Jesus means savior. But if we were to be more literal, we would say: "He will *liberate* his people from their sins." The Old Testament cry of liberation breaks through in the name Jesus—as it does in the older spelling of Joshua, or Jeshua. Jesus means "liberator."

The word "savior" means this in Greek as well as it did in Hebrew. The angel of Luke 2:11 is really saying: "Unto you this day is born a Liberator." We can sense this meaning wherever Jesus is called Savior. The combinations Jesus Christ and Lord Jesus are familiar, but we never hear of Jesus Savior (except in Acts 13:23, but then Luke was not a Jew). This would be superfluous, for Jesus *means* Savior, as any Jew would know. What sense would it make to say Liberator Liberator? If one wants to say Liberator, he can just say Jesus.

But in the New Testament the meaning of "liberation" is much broader than it is in the Old. The entire, all-embracing work of Jesus Christ is wrapped up in that one word. This includes all "things in heaven and things on earth" (Eph. 1:10).

Reconciliation is liberation too. It is a liberation out of the power and bondage of sin into the freedom of God's sons. God, too—not only Jesus—is praised as Savior in the New Testament (Luke 1:47; I Tim. 1:1; 2:3; 4:10). That God should be called Liberator along with Jesus is certainly not surprising. He has always been the Liberator, the Savior, and never so clearly and finally as when He sends His only Son (Titus 3:4).

20
Sin

With "sin" we have on our hands a word that is easy to translate and has not been seriously misshapen by theological prejudices, but which has been worn thin both by excessive use and by misuse.

What do the Bible writers mean by "sin" and "sinning"? Well, let's begin with an obvious and general remark. "Sin" is a religious word; its meaning is determined by religious associations. It is not a moralistic notion. This means that sin is a lot more than breaking rules that human beings make up. To be human assumes a relationship with God, and this assumption keeps us from letting human customs, manners, and morals have the last word about man's behavior—to say nothing of having the last word about man's deepest reality. It is in this sense that sin means much more than bad morals, and why the word "sin" is not a moralistic word.

But let's not go too far. We have said that "sin" cannot be defined moralistically; we have not said that sin has nothing to do with morality. Sin does break out in the arena of morals. This is biblical.

The Bible uses several words for sin, but all of them point to the actual comings and goings of real people.

The most common word for sin in the Old Testament can be translated "misdeed," a failure to hit the mark. The story of the Benjamite stone-throwers, seven hundred of them, illustrates this literal meaning of sin. These wonderful left-handed stone-throwers reported in Judges 20 never missed; they were always on target within "a hair's breadth." A sinful act is an act that misses the mark. What mark? The answer to that lies in the basic form of life within the covenant partnership, the form which is the standard for all relations between men and God, and which in turn is the standard for all human relations. What misses the mark is any act that does not fit into the covenant relationship.

From this comes the Old Testament expression "sinning toward (or against) God," or "toward (or against) a brother." Consider Genesis 20:6, Exodus 10:16, Judges 11:27, and Jeremiah 37:18. The same thing comes out in the New Testament, as Luke 15:18 and 21 illustrates. To be truly human means to live as a covenant partner; and covenant partnership is realized concretely in good acts. Thus, being a sinner amounts to acting in a way that misses what *human* actions ought to achieve. The sinner is, in that sense, a creature who has missed the mark of humanity; being a sinner means he has failed to do and be what is basic to human life. He is a caricature of the covenant-partner man.

This leads to another word for sin in the Bible, one that hits precisely at this anti-covenantal character of sin. To the Israelite the strongest word for sin is "unrighteousness." Unrighteousness is what ruins the covenant relationship. But if unrighteousness ruins the covenant, it also ruins the unrighteous person, for covenant life is the only real human life. The Old Testament says this in various graphic ways. For example, "The Lord has returned the evil-doing of Nabal upon his own head" (I Sam. 25:39; see also I Kings 2:32, 44; Pss. 94:23; 9:16; and Prov. 5:22). Unrighteousness is a boomerang.

If we want to talk about sin the way the Bible talks about it, we have to include sin's consequences. But the consequences of sin do not *follow* acts of sin, as "b" follows "a." The consequences come as part of the package. Sin is a complex whole. It is like a snowball that gets bigger as it rolls down a slope, or like a rock that is set loose at the top of a deep ravine and catches snow as it rolls down—we don't know how big it will become until it reaches the bottom of the mountain. It may become an avalanche. Sin and decay, sin and guilt cling together so closely that sometimes the word "unrighteousness" has to be translated to include all of these elements. Sometimes it is translated as "iniquity," and in a way this includes not only the immediate act, but the guilt of it as well (Exod. 20:5). Sometimes the word "iniquity" concentrates on sin and its corrupting effects (see Gen. 19:15—King James).

Another Old Testament word for sin means rebellion, the violation of a vow, a trespass. Sin is an act that violates a covenant relationship. Genesis 31:36 provides an example: "And Jacob was wroth, and chode with Laban: and Jacob answered and said to Laban, What is my trespass? what is my sin, that thou hast so hotly pursued me?" Amos and Micah are striking in their judgment on trespasses against social justice, acts they characterize as breaking the covenant (Amos 1:3, 9; 3:14; 5:12; Mic. 1:5; 3:8).

The Old Testament has a larger vocabulary for sin than the words we have mentioned here. But these three pretty well sum up what it means in the other cases. In the New Testament, the same lexicon for sin appears. For example, I John 3:4 characterizes sin as unrighteousness, and thus as a combination of misdeed, guilt, and ruin. But there is a two-fold difference in the way the New Testament approaches the concept of sin.

In the first place, the New Testament thinks more broadly than does the Old Testament. This is because Jesus Christ, the Liberator and Propitiator, has come. Where He appears, a larger light is thrown on the reality of the sin from which He frees men. Indeed, John 15:22 tells us that sin really first came to light when Christ came to expose it.

The second way in which the New Testament approach

to the concept of sin differs from that of the Old Testament is that the New Testament thinks of sin as a power. For Paul sin is not so much a quality of a person as a power to which he is subject. Sin reigns and men are bond slaves of it (e.g., Rom. 5:21; 6:14; 6:16; and 7:14). Of course it is a matter of actions too (Rom. 5:15-19). But it is the kind of action that grabs hold of men and makes prisoners of them. Sin has grim proportions. John stresses this: "He who commits sin is of the devil" (I John 3:8). This is the ultimate background of human sin. Sin destroys human life, as the Devil has been "a murderer from the beginning" (John 8:44).

21
The Son of Man (I)

The name Jesus tells us what the Lord came to us for. We saw that He came to liberate us—this is what "Jesus" means.

But Jesus has other names as well, and each of those names tells us something of its own about His message and His work. Perhaps the most remarkable of all is the name Son of man. It appears only in the Gospel writers, where Jesus uses it almost eighty times. In fact, He seems to have liked this name better than any other—better than the title Christ, for example. When Peter confesses that Jesus is the Christ (or Messiah) in Mark 8:29, Jesus does not repeat that title when He speaks in verse 31. Instead He speaks of Himself as the Son of man. Even stranger is the fact that no one else addresses Him by the name He evidently prefers. Furthermore, it is used in only three places outside the four Gospels: Acts 7:56 and Revelation 1:13 and

14:14. It is just the other way around with the title Christ.
Jesus seldom uses it. The later Bible writers use it more
than any other.

Why does the name Son of man gradually fade out of
use? Why does the church hardly ever use it? Was it that its
meaning was lost on others? Perhaps.

The name comes from the Old Testament, and out of a
rather ordinary setting. People are always being identified
as "the son of so and so." Or when the Old Testament
writer wants to point to a man's role or to some aspect of
his character he may say something like this: So and so are
"sons of oil"—as a literal translation of Zechariah 4:14
reads. What Zechariah means is that these men (the two
olive branches in the vision) are anointed. Ephesians 2:2
refers to the "sons of disobedience." I Peter 1:14 speaks
literally of "sons of obedience." A son of something or
other is a person whose character is marked by that of
which he is called a son.

What, then, is a son of man? The simplest answer is this:
he is a man whose character is marked by manhood, or
humanness. The Old Testament gives us examples of this
definition. For instance: "What is man that thou art mind-
ful of him, and the son of man that thou dost care for
him?" (Ps. 8:4). The same thought is present in Psalm
80:17. To be a man and to be a son of man are about the
same things.

The simplest thing for us to do, then, is to suppose that
this is about all Jesus meant when He called Himself the
Son of man. That is, we could conclude that He meant to
tell us that He was really a human being, just as we mean
that He is really God when we call Him the Son of God.

But we should not jump to this conclusion yet. There is
a rather strange passage in the Old Testament in which the
son of a man is of a very special sort. I am referring to
Daniel 7:13 ff. Daniel sees in a vision a figure "like a son
of man" who is coming "with the clouds of heaven" to
receive lordship and kingly power from "the Ancient of

Days." The Jewish (and the New Testament) expectation
of the Kingdom of God is closely tied to this vision: One
day, at the end of time, the Kingdom will come because
the great King shall establish His divine lordship on earth.
The Son of man is this great king. He is going to erect the
Kingdom, and His lordship will never end (Dan. 7:14;
Luke 1:33). This can mean only one thing: Jesus calls
Himself the Son of man to tell us that the end-time has
come, and that He Himself is the King of that glorious
time.

Jesus' way of using the name fits the associations Daniel
provides for it, for whenever He calls Himself the Son of
man, He points to the end-time. See, for example, Luke
17:22, where we read about "the 'days of the Son of
man.' " See also Matthew 24:27 and 24:37 ff. Furthermore, recall how Jesus talks in Mark 8:38 about His
coming "in glory with his holy angels" and in Mark 14:62
about the Son of man as "coming with the clouds of
heaven." (Note the parallel with Daniel 7:13.) Clearly,
Jesus calls Himself the Son of man to tell us that He is the
One who will come (Matt. 11:3) to bring in the Kingdom.
His great origin and His great status are both underscored
by the name Son of man.

This is why the name Son of man and the final judgment belong together. Look at John 5:27: God "has given
him authority to execute judgment, *because he is the Son
of man.*" And, finally, read Matthew 25:31-46: The Son of
man is the King of glory—the King, or Judge, or Protector,
or Liberator of the poor.

So we have a surprising conclusion. "Son of man" seems
to indicate the lowly state of the incarnate Lord, His
humanity, His being a man among men. But more basically
the name points in precisely the other direction. It is
almost the highest title that can be given Jesus. In it He
unveils His greatness, His kingliness.

Only after we see the exalted direction in which "Son of
man" points can we appreciate the strange way in which

this king comes to us—so very different from the way kings usually come. That is, only when we see that Jesus really means to say something great about Himself can we truly appreciate the fact that "Son of man" *also* indicates something humble. This leads us to the next chapter.

22
The Son of Man (II)

We have seen that "Son of man" means royalty, heavenly greatness. The Son of man represents the coming Kingdom; He is the one with "all authority in heaven and on earth" (Matt. 28:18). But now we must notice that the name Son of man appears in contexts that have nothing to do with the King and His coming in glory at the end of time. These are places that speak instead of His suffering and dying.

We no more than hear that the Son of man will usher in the Kingdom (the glory of the Father) than we also hear that very shortly "the Son of man will be delivered up to be crucified" (Matt. 25:31 ff. and 26:2). To be the Son of man and to be a suffering man coincide. The way Jesus demonstrates that He is the King is the way of suffering and dying. He is the Lord, but a servant kind of Lord. Many verses in the New Testament support this point. Consider, for example, Mark 10:45: "For the Son of man also came not to be served but to serve, and to give his life as a ransom for many." See, too, such passages as Mark 8:31; 9:31; and 10:33. Paul also makes this connection crystal clear in Philippians 2: He emptied Himself, and therefore God has highly exalted Him. This is the unbroken thread of the New Testament witness to Jesus

Christ, a thread that remains the same even though it has many colors. "Was it not necessary that the Christ should suffer these things and enter into his glory?" (Luke 24:26).

But we have one more thing to note, something that goes back to what we said at the beginning. "Son of man!" means, literally, nothing more than "man." We should not forget this simplest point. The One who has all power in heaven and on earth is *man.* Again, the One who goes through suffering to glory is *man.* The Gospel of Jesus Christ can be understood in this way, that Jesus is representative of us men. Jesus is *the man* in the sense that He, the one man, stands in the place of all men together.

So "Son of man" does not mean only that Jesus and the Kingdom belong together, nor only that Jesus and suffering servanthood belong together, but also that Jesus and manhood belong together. When we confess that Jesus is Lord, and when we confess that Jesus is the Suffering Servant, we mean to confess that Jesus is Lord on behalf of us *all* and that He is Servant on behalf of us *all.*

The Scriptures taken at face value clearly tell us this. In Daniel 7:13, the lordship is given to a single person, the Son of man. But in verse 18, not just a single person but many persons receive the lordship. "But the saints of the Most High shall receive the kingdom, and possess the kingdom for ever, for ever and ever." The One, the Son of man, is the leader (Acts 3:15), the "pioneer and perfecter" (Heb. 12:2), and the representative of the whole people. He is the substitute, the place-taker, for all the rest. His way is their way; His glory is their glory; His exaltation means the exaltation of all.

This is the same pattern as that of the Servant, for He is the substitute sufferer also. The one Servant represents the whole people. He suffers and is punished for all the others. This is the reason Jesus calls Himself the Son of man. This is the true sign that the equation is He equals We.

Now, by way of parenthesis, notice the remarkable

words of Matthew 24:40: "Truly, I say to you, as you did it to one of the least of these my brethren, you did it to me." This, we are told, is what the *Son of man* will say (vs. 31). We could hardly find a clearer witness to the equation that He equals We, the Son of man equals Men. Jesus, in this case, even reverses the equation: *They* equal Me.

Hebrews 2:6 ff., which quotes the passage from Psalm 8 that sings of the glory of man, is related to the equation. It is true, the writer of Hebrews acknowledges, that "we do not yet see everything in subjection to him [man]." But we do see Jesus, first as Servant and then as King and Lord. Jesus is the man who has come into glory—the son of man from Psalm 8, *the* man. The others will get their glory in and through Him.

Finally, as we read about the second Adam in I Corinthians 15:45 (and in Rom. 5:12 ff.), we see that we have the same thought. Paul is speaking of Jesus as *the* man (Adam), our representative and substitute—though now in glory. That is, as He is now, so shall we be in the future. "Just as we have borne the image of the man of dust, we shall also bear the image of the man of heaven" (I Cor. 15:49).

23
The One and the Many

The meaning of these words seems perfectly clear. But we must talk about them because they have a background that is not at all transparent.

We have on our hands here something that may have struck us while we were considering the name Son of man—the matter of substitution. This, at least, is the way theology often puts it. The word is clear enough, but it has one shortcoming. It sounds just a bit mechanical. Yet the Bible does not make it sound mechanical at all. Moreover, the notion of substitution, as we ordinarily think of it, appears in the Bible with a great many more variations than we usually allow for.

The concept of the one and the many is applied to all sorts of relationships. For instance, one member of a given group can stand for the entire group, and vice versa. Take one example: The Bible writers often mention just one part of the body when they really mean the entire person. Job says: "My kidneys sorely long . . ." (Job 19:27). What he means is that *he*—his whole being—sorely longs. The one organ stands for the whole man. Similar instances are multiplied in the Bible. Man is spoken of in terms of the heart, the liver, the soul, the spirit, even the hand. Each of these parts stands for the whole (as if they were substitutes).

Taken as a body, man is apparently such a unity that we cannot grab hold of a part without having our hands on the whole of him. Paul seizes on this to make a point about the Body of Christ when he says that the whole body suffers when one member suffers (I Cor. 12). Paul is talking here, of course, about a human fellowship: individuals are limbs of a body, members of a fellowship. A society of people, the people of Israel for instance, can be represented by one person—the one can stand for the many.

But does this body-like unity really reflect our experience? It did for the Israelite. He did not experience his humanity as individualistically as we tend to do. The unity of the fellowship was not just a slogan, a manner of speaking. It was part of his deepest consciousness; it defined his actions and his very being. The entire Israelite community was a large "I." It was an "I" that repeated itself in the thousands of other "I" 's within the single

Israel. Each of the little "I" 's bore the same stamp as did the large "I" of the community.

Take one example: In Numbers 20:19, we read that the Israelites said to Edom: "We will go up by the highway; and if we drink of your water, *I* and my cattle, then *I* will pay for it." The "we" is something of a large "I." And alternatively the "I" is represented a thousand-fold in every single Israelite. So we can see that for the Israelites it would not sound strange to hear that the many are represented by the one, and that the one bears the many within him.

The king is naturally the one figure who most clearly stands for the whole people; in a sense, he *is* the people. When David sinned by making a census of the people (II Sam. 24), the whole people were punished with him. This is hardly fair in our eyes. But it seems unfair only until we understand that the king and the people are related as the one and the many. He *is* the people. The people are involved in what he does, and are punished with him. They do not, in fact, stand aloof from his acts. They are considered to be a single mind; indeed, they are one in mind unless they actually *demonstrate* the contrary.

The unity of the one and the many embraces both the past and the future. Looking backward, we come upon the ancestor of Israel, Jacob. The Bible constantly speaks of Jacob (or his other name, Israel) when it really means the whole people that come from him. The same goes for Moab; the Israelites encounter the Moabite people, but they are said to encounter Moab the man. And the Edomites are simply called Edom (Num. 20:18).

Let's go backward a step further. All the way back to Adam. With him too we have the one man who stands for the whole—for the whole of us men. Translated literally, "Adam" means nothing other than man, or mankind, and appears to us this way some 600 times in the Old Testament.

Could this help us to understand Genesis 1-3 and Romans 5:12 ff. a bit better? To speak of one's ancestor is to speak of all the generations that followed. This was self-evident to Paul, a man whose language was forged in a Jewish setting. We *are* Adam and unless someone can demonstrate that he is different from the rest of us, everyone is included. But who *can* show that he is really different?

The connection between members of a society also extends forward in time. This is suggested in the second law of the Decalogue, where God says He will deal with the third and fourth generations in the same way as with the person guilty of this particular evil (Exod. 20:5). Here again, it is assumed that the following generations will be of one mind and feeling, and this is why they are included in the punishment. They are not mechanically thrust into the guilt of the one person. The Old Testament knows that the children should not die because of the sins of the fathers (Jer. 31:30; Ezek. 18:1 ff.). But they must *demonstrate* that they are different.

One last example. Isaiah 53 points out that the one Servant shall "make many to be accounted righteous" (vs. 11). Here we have the terms with which we began: the one and the many. The New Testament introduces the words into the celebration of the Supper: "the blood poured out for many" (Matt. 26:28). And let's not overlook Romans 5:12-19. Paul gives us a refrain here, with almost every verse repeating it: the One (Servant) who went the route of obedience for us all—He is We.

The mystery of Jesus Christ cannot be understood without the Old Testament vision of the one and the many. For He has come, the New Testament proclaims, and so we must receive Him as the One who substitutes for the many. His humiliation is ours. His glorification is ours. To speak about Jesus is to speak about us men. Only if we demonstrate the contrary, by our unbelief and disobedience, can we break the connection.

24
Election Means Preference

"Election" is the most offensive word in the vocabulary of the church! Its very offensiveness compels us to take a hard look at it. What is the connection between this word and the total message of the Bible? And if we are offended by it, are we offended by God's preferences or by our misunderstanding of election?

First something about the word "preference." This is without doubt the basic sense of the word "election," at least in the Old Testament. Genesis 29:30 tells us that Jacob loved Rachel more than Leah. But in the next verse we are told that he hated Leah. To love, here, means to prefer someone. To hate seems to mean not to prefer someone. Jacob prefers Rachel; he does not prefer Leah (see I Sam. 1:5 for a comparable instance).

We have to see these words as part of the whole Old Testament word-picture; we have to hear the whole story if we are to understand the bits and pieces of it. For instance, Jesus does not mean to tell us in Luke 14:26 that we really ought to hate our mothers and fathers—not as *we* think of hate. Again, it is a question of preference. Matthew suggests the sense, in his rendering of the same statement: "He who loves father or mother *more* than me is not worthy of me" (Matt. 10:37). Malachi 1:2, 3 has to be read the same way: " 'I have loved you,' says the Lord. But you say, 'How hast thou loved us?' 'Is not Esau Jacob's brother?' says the Lord. 'Yet I loved Jacob and I hated Esau.' "

The notion of preference provides the content of the word "election." A Hebrew dictionary tells us this; but so do the many places in the Old Testament where "to love more than" and to "choose out" are parallels (Deut. 4:37; 7:8; 10:15, etc.). To elect means to have preference for. It is in this sense that Israel is the elect people. They are the people of God's preference (Amos 3:2; Ps. 147:19, 20).

The main issue of the Bible's message of God's election is not what we sometimes call predestination. It is rather God's preference, as He brings it to light. But is this democratic of God, to prefer one people? Does the word "preference" soften the blow; is not preference about the same thing as arbitrary choice?

To answer this question we have to keep our Bible open. We should ask ourselves *whom* it is that God prefers. We can best get at this by reading the story of Jesus Christ, for He stands in our midst as *the* representative of this God who has preferences. Anyone who has seen Him at work has seen God Himself at work (John 14:9).

For whom does Jesus Christ show preference? Is it not clear on every page of the Gospels? He prefers the lost, the publicans and sinners, the sick and rejected. In a word He prefers all those in need of His saving hand. We *can* describe God's preferences: they are preached to us in the whole Bible, and preached with great force and clarity. Notice that I said *preached*. The notion is not swept under a rug somewhere. To put it boldly, though without exaggeration, the preaching of the Gospel is the same as the preaching of God's preference. Anyone who does not have a feeling for this has not grasped the point of the Gospel. He is something of a Pharisee. To the Pharisee Jesus' preferences were offensive; he forgot how to understand Israel's God and thus he could not understand Jesus as God's representative.

The preference of God—Jesus let us see what it was like; He witnessed to it in all His words and actions. What He told us comes to this: God's preference means that He is a merciful God and intends to stay that way. We get a glimpse of His manner of being God, His "style" (as G. C. Berkouwer puts it), by looking at His election (His having preferences). He does not want to exercise His Godness except by showing Godly mercy. This is why we cannot get close to God "on the basis of works." This is why we can get close to Him only as He (in His bottomless mercy) calls us (Rom. 9:11).

This is the golden thread that binds Romans 9 together. Paul is not dealing with the question of the *pre*-destiny of some individuals; he is revealing God's preferences. Why should Isaac be chosen instead of Ishmael; why Jacob instead of Esau? It is because God wanted to maintain His style, Paul says; that is, it is not that one man is better or older than another that qualifies him for God's preference. God's mercy alone accounts for it. A man is a Christian by the grace of God, not by His Christian accomplishments. To put it another way, partnership in the covenant rests in election.

The purpose of preaching election is made quite clear in the Scriptures. First, one begins to praise God when he knows God's preference (His election), for one praises when he discovers mercy. Our standing with God rests in Christ alone: "He that glorieth, let him glory in the Lord" (I Cor. 1:31—King James). We can be part of God's program—this is almost incredible!

The Psalms of Israel are rooted deep in an awareness of God's preference. So are the songs of praise we find in the New Testament. We begin to sing when we discover that we Gentiles share with Israel in God's covenant promise (Eph. 3:6; Acts 11:18; Rom. 11:33-36).

The other side of God's preference is this: We can take part only as people who have no right to take part—and who know it. The preaching of God's preference is humbling to hear. It brings us to our knees; it makes us hold out our hands and implore that we too be allowed to take part (see Matt. 15:21-28 and Luke 7:1-10).

This is what the Pharisees could not swallow. Were they not allowed to take part? Naturally they were. They were *called* to take part. But they had to come in the same way—humbly, modestly, like the shy woman of Matthew 15. They had to ask, as a child asks: "If you please."

The real offense taken at the preference of God lies here—not in an intellectual notion of something like fatalism. To read fatalism into God's election can happen only through a serious misunderstanding of the Bible. It is not as though we cannot know where we stand with God. The proclamation of God's preference tells us that we can know, and know exactly, where we stand with God. The fatalism that has now and then crept into the church's talk about God rises out of another place: it comes out of the question of whether God's sovereign power and our free will can fit together. Are these not two exclusive notions that contradict each other? They are indeed to anyone who will not hold up his hands to ask.

But what do I have to fear from God's preference once I have discovered what that preference is all about? Once we know what sort of people He prefers, His sovereign power becomes our blessedness. This is what Paul tells us in Ephesians 1:3-6.

25
The Soul

Few words of Holy Scripture have been more misunderstood in the course of history than the word "soul." Our story would be too long if we tried to trace the sources of these misunderstandings. Instead we will ask straight off, How do the writers of the Bible use the word? What do they want to tell us and what do they not want to tell us? To begin with the last question, they do not mean what we usually mean; they do not mean to point to an invisible thing inside our bodies. This is what the soul came to mean in the history of the church—a higher sort of essence, higher because it was more like God. And this "essence" was set apart from the body, which was a lower sort of thing, lower because its fleshly, earthly sort of stuff was further from God.

The Bible writers would not recognize this way of talking about the soul. Man does not appear in the Bible as the sum of two separate parts, the higher plus the lower, the soul as the real man plus the body as a temporary piece of baggage that can be dispensed with. Man comes off the pages of the Bible as a unity, a whole that cannot be divided into two parts. The real man is the concrete, tangible, whole person. Separate words for the components of man, the parts out of which the whole is constructed, are not provided. If the Israelite wants to point to the whole man, he does not do anything like add up his parts. He points to one organ or part that *stands* for the whole. We saw examples of this in the chapter on the one and the many.

This means that we will do well to read the word "soul" differently than we have gotten used to. The Bible writers use the word "soul" for what makes a living being alive— the primeval vitality that resides in the blood (Lev. 17:14).

A surprising thing about this biblical way of talking about the soul is that it is used of animals (Gen. 1:20) as well as of people (Gen. 2:7). Man was created a "living soul"—or living being—but the animals were created this way too. The earth crawls with living souls (Gen. 1:20). Even God has a soul (Lev. 26:11, 30; Judg. 10:16). "Soul" is a word with enormous compass.

The word "soul," it should be noticed, does not indicate a blank aliveness, but an active, emotional, responsive life. This explains why plants do not have souls; they merely vegetate. The "soul" hungers for meat (Deut. 12:16), loathes manna (Num. 21:5), hates some things (II Sam. 5:8) and is enamored of others. These are all emotional words. Vitality apparently amounts to being able to respond, to being emotionally alive. This too stretches the meaning of "soul."

But we have not yet noted the important part. In the examples we have given, the phrase is usually "my soul" or "our soul." Sometimes this is translated weakly as simply "I" or "we." For the word "soul" comes down to this. Someone's soul is very much himself; "my soul" usually means "me," the person I am in all my special characteristics—alive and vital. We meet this manner of speech in the Psalms, an example being Psalm 116:4—"O Lord . . . deliver my soul" (King James). The poet does not have his mind here on something like an immortal soul, as we call it. Nor is he dramatizing the forgiveness of sins, important as this is. The context helps us see the point. He simply means "save my life" or "save me." The soul is the vital, living person himself. And when the Bible talks of God's soul, it simply means the living God Himself.

With this, we are back at one of the first discoveries we made, that the word "soul" applies to God as well as to men and animals. The difference between God and man (or animal)—at least in this connection—is not that Jahweh has no soul while men and animals do have souls. The difference is deeper: Man's vital existence is dependent on God (see Gen. 2:7; Ps. 104:29). A man cannot keep his own soul alive (Ps. 22:29); one day he dies. His "soul" is poured out into death as water is poured on the ground (II Sam. 14:14; Isa. 53:12). In brief, Jahweh alone is free from death; the soul of man dies.

We have seen enough to understand that the Bible surely has something else in mind with "soul" than a higher component of man, the part that does not die—a spiritual thing in distinction from a dying physical body. If we come to the Bible and insist on putting our meaning for "soul" in what we read, we will simply never understand what the Bible says about it.

We don't have to adopt all of the Bible's way of talking

about the soul; talking about the "soul in the blood" is not going to help us in our day. But we can recapture the intent. We can think of man as whole and integrated; we can avoid splitting him into a higher and lower being. We can do this because we know that God made His covenant with whole, physical-spiritual, concrete men—not with immortal souls. What we want to learn from the Bible is what the concrete being called man, as a whole, ought or ought not do as a covenant partner with God. To eliminate the body-life of man from real humanity is a form of inhumanity to man; and that is surely unbiblical.

26
Body and Limbs

The Old Testament does not have a word for body. Translations sometimes use the word "body," but it is not found in the Hebrew text. How can we account for this strange lapse? In the last chapter we saw that the Bible writers refused to split a man up between soul and body, between the higher (spiritual) and the lower (physical) halves. We saw how the Bible likes to take man whole and treat him that way. So the words we find useful to make our division—body and soul—are not needed in the biblical vocabulary. At least this is true of the Old Testament. We will have to take a look at the New.

Maybe we should ask ourselves, What do we mean by the whole man in his concrete existence? To answer, we can look back at the early chapters of this book. The concrete man is man doing his deeds and speaking his words. The concrete man is always the body-man, but the body-man in action, occupied with his neighbor, with things, or with God. The Israelite never got it into his head that a kind of unembodied human being could exist; this comes out clearly in the large role that the limbs (the "members," as the New Testament would put it) and the organs of the human body play in the biblical language.

Take the word "hand" for instance. It is used often in both the Old and New Testaments, and of both man and God. Recall Psalm 80:17: "But let thy hand be upon the man of thy right hand." And there is the expression that speaks of giving someone or something over "into someone's hands" (see, e.g., Gen. 9:2; Lev. 26:25; Judg. 15:12). The biblical writers have more in mind than a naked hand with five fingers; they mean the hand-in-action. "The Lord's strong right hand" refers to God's strong help—His helping hands. We have the same thing with God's ears. The Psalmist is pointing to God's willingness to listen to our cries. The same goes for His eyes (Pss. 94:9; 33:18).

Similarly, when we read about being "delivered over into the hands of an enemy," this is not to stress hands as such, but to call up the thought of what the enemy can do with his hands—make us captive, push us down, and the like. In a word, to mention the hand or any other part of one's body is for the Bible writer to point to a typical function of that limb. The name of the limb is used, but its typical function is intended. Now our conclusion: The writers of the Bible always think of the concrete, embodied, functioning man. They never think of a ghost inside a body. They refer to the limbs and organs because man is man in his handling and his hands, his walking and his feet, his speaking and his tongue, his seeing and his eyes.

Now on to the New Testament. Here we do meet the word "body," and sometimes in passages that do indeed want to stress the difference between the inner and outer aspect of man. The Old Testament makes the same distinction, but it does it simply by using such words as "heart." Matthew 10:28 uses the word "body" this way: "And do not fear those who kill the body but cannot kill the soul; rather fear him who can destroy both soul and body in hell." But there are passages that are more important to the biblical witness and our understanding of it. Paul leads us into a very crucial consideration of the body. What does Paul mean by it?

In many instances the word "body" denotes the whole man in all his limbs and organs and functioning concretely in words and deeds. Let's take Romans 6:12-13 as an example: "Let not sin therefore reign in your mortal bodies"; and a bit further on, "Do not yield your members to sin as instruments of wickedness"; and finally, "Yield yourselves to God." The body is made up of members, and what we are to understand by "members" we learned from the Old Testament; they are the organs of the body not as such, but in their functioning. By "members" Paul means the whole man as he is, a man in action. The apostle goes on to identify "bodies" and "members" with "yourselves." "Body" equals "members" equals "self." When Paul at the end of verse 13 reverts back to "members," he might equally well have said "body"—as in fact he does in Romans 12:1 (see also Rom. 6:19 and 7:5, as well as Col. 3:5—King James).

We haven't really finished with Paul and his use of the word "body." But a lot has been said. Consider the imagery that Paul uses in I Corinthians 12, where he speaks of the church as Christ's Body (see also Rom. 12:4 ff. and Eph. 4:25 and 5:30). Paul uses the words "members" and "body" because among other reasons he wants to stress the concrete actions that people in the congregation perform towards each other. To be a member is to be in action.

This much is perfectly clear: Paul never uses the word "body" in opposition to the soul. The man who is called by God is a concrete, embodied man. Anyone who minimizes the corporal side of man does something the Bible never does. (Minimize the body, and you have to minimize something of the resurrection of Christ.) To be redeemed is not to be redeemed from the body, but to be liberated as a whole, body-concrete person (Rom. 8:23).

27
Flesh and Spirit

The words "flesh" and "spirit" are familiar to anyone who has dipped even shallowly into the New Testament. One cannot get far into Paul without running into the apostle's vivid contrasts between them (see, e.g., Gal. 5:13-26; Rom. 8:1-17). But the meanings of both words are so varied that we can hardly do more here than skim the surface of them. We will limit ourselves to one question: Why are flesh and spirit opposed to each other? Or are they?

In the Old Testament the word "flesh" is often used simply for the meat that we eat (e.g., Num. 11:13). On the other hand, when the writers speak of men as flesh, we know they have something rather special in mind.

But we must be careful here. They do not mean to put flesh over against or alongside the soul. We should utterly misunderstand them if we forced that thought into their heads. True, man has flesh, just as animals do. The Old Testament, as we have seen, does not use the word "body." For the Israelite, man *is* flesh—the whole man is flesh. This explains why such expressions as "my flesh" simply mean "myself" as a human being (see, e.g., Pss. 16:9; 84:2). The phrase "all flesh" is the same as "all men" (Gen. 6:12; Jer. 45:5; Joel 2:28).

So "flesh" means the *person,* all of him. But beyond this it means the weak person, the man who is fragile and only temporary. "All men are flesh" means "Men come and go." "All flesh is grass" (Isa. 40:6)—this is what the Bible writers want to say. Grass lives and dies. Men, being flesh, also live and die; to be flesh means to live at the borders of death. Weakness is the accent we hear. To recall another familiar text: "Cursed is the man who trusts in man and makes flesh his arm, whose heart turns away from the Lord" (Jer. 17:5). To be a man is to be flesh, and to be flesh is to be powerless.

The biblical antonym for "flesh" is "spirit." As "flesh" stands for weakness, "spirit" stands for power. Look at Isaiah 31:3: "The Egyptians are men, and not God; and their horses are flesh, and not spirit." Here it is: "Flesh" means weak and "spirit" means strong. But there is something else at work here. As men and flesh go together, so God and spirit go together. The real source of power does not lie with the so-called "powerful," but with God—that is, with His Spirit, as Zechariah 4:6 says.

Now then, we are ready to go on to the New Testament, particularly to Paul. Here, flesh and spirit seem to stand over against each other as two hostile forces, two warring powers—like light and darkness in John. How does Paul come to this?

For Paul, as for the Old Testament, flesh is a definitive characteristic of human beings—flesh means that man is fragile, weak, mortal. But Paul goes beyond this. The word "flesh" also points to man in his emaciated condition with respect to the things of God, particularly in his understanding of God (Gal. 1:16). "Flesh" means that man cannot stand before God innocently (Rom. 3:20) and cannot inherit the Kingdom (I Cor. 15:50). More bluntly, since man is flesh he always lets himself become the slave of the flesh (Phil. 3:3). The flesh becomes for Paul a power of sorts, a power beyond man's control, a power to which man surrenders—just as he does to the law and to death. This appears more clearly when Paul sets another power over against the power of the flesh—the power of the

Spirit. This Spirit is not some inner source of human power. Paul is talking about an influential power beyond man into which men enter when they are liberated from the power of the flesh.

What sort of new sphere of influence is this? Paul tells us clearly in II Corinthians 3:17. First he says that "the Lord [Jesus Christ] is the Spirit." The new sphere of influence is the lordship of Jesus Christ. The apostle then goes on to point out that "where the Spirit of the Lord is, there is freedom." When a man is taken into the sphere of the Spirit, he can breathe freely again. He can live again as a free person.

To get what Paul means in even sharper focus, we have to read Galatians 5:13-26. To live "by the Spirit" (vs. 16) means to stand in freedom (vs. 13), which means to serve each other in love (vs. 13b). And if we are to get an inkling of how deep and broad Paul views the contrast between Spirit and flesh, we must study Romans 8:1-17.

One thing becomes clear to us negatively. The contrast between flesh and spirit is not a conflict between a higher and a lower part of man—or between the invisible spirit of man and his physical body. Perhaps this comes out most clearly in I Corinthians 15:44 and 45. Paul talks here of a "natural body" and a "spiritual body." This unique combination ("spiritual body") forecloses on any notion of spirit as an enemy of body. For Paul the body is nothing less than man, the specific, concrete, active person. This is the man who will share in the resurrection (I Cor. 15:44) and then be freed forever from the demands of the flesh.

Now, let us add one more thought. The lusts of the flesh (Gal. 5:19-25) are not merely physical impulses. The same things that Paul calls the "lusts of the flesh" he calls the "lusts of the heart" in Romans 1:24.

We are dealing here with the whole man, and with the crucial question of where his deepest allegiances are, whom and what he serves. The question is whether he is going to be a prisoner of his own (pious or impious) alienation from

God (that is, whether he is going to "live after the flesh")
or whether he is going to live as a free man, playing
joyfully in the sphere of influence created by Jesus Christ.

28
The Name

When the Bible writers talk about "the name of God"
they mean simply God Himself. Why do they do this? Why
don't they just say "God"? To answer this, we shall have
to talk a bit about the notion of names in general.

As we know, the Bible put a lot more weight on names
than we do. In fact, most ancient cultures did. We use
names (unless we happen to be in love) merely as identification labels to paste on people. We choose a particular
name because we like its sound or because it is the name of
someone we love or admire, but we almost never take into
account the meaning of the name. The function of names
is merely to help us keep one person apart from another.
The Israelite felt differently about names. Of course he too
used names to distinguish one person from another. But
the difference is this: He also meant his names to focus on
the basic qualities that distinguished a person. Among us a
name usually does not tell us anything about a person
(unless it happens to be a nickname that attaches to a
superficial peculiarity, like "Red" or "Freckles"). A man
whose name is Fisher is not expected to earn his living on
the sea. In Israel, on the other hand, a man would get the
name Fisher only if he really was a fisher. The name, in
short, really did tell people something about a man, something that distinguished him as an individual among the
many. Thus if one attacked the name of a person, he

attacked the person himself. The name of a man *was* the
man—a man's name stood for what the man stood for
among his fellow men. To take just one example, Jahweh
promised Abram in Genesis 12:2 that He would make
Abram's *name* great. But this meant, of course, that He
would make Abram great. The name is the man.

We begin, then, to catch on to what the Bible writers
meant by "the name of the Lord" or just "the Name."
Something festive comes through in the expression. For
what sort of faith would Israel have had if it had believed
only that there was *something* above them—some unknown or vaguely known higher power? Their pagan neighbors believed as much. As long as you do not really know
that higher power personally, as long as you are not in on
what He is really like and really wants, you don't know His
name. And that means you don't know Him. That sort of
nameless faith is more like terror. There is nothing festive in
it at all.

But when God tells people His name, terror vanishes and
a real relationship begins. This is how it was between God
and Israel. At the very beginning Israel received a revelation of the *Name.* That is, God told Israel who and what
He is (Exod. 3:13 ff.). True, He did this in a rather
roundabout way. "I shall go with you, and you will find
out who I am"—this seems to be the sense of verse 14. The
name seems to reveal God, but with a veil still covering
Him. Yet, the veil does not actually hide Him; it really
underscores His authentic Godness. He is the God of the
covenant; and to reveal Himself as the God of the covenant
He must keep Himself free from any human domination,
any human control, that might twist Him into something
like the gods and powers of the religious world around
Israel. A god made by man can never be a creative Covenant Partner. God wants to keep the way open toward the
future, a way that leaves Him free to bring more surprises
to His covenant partners (Gen. 32:29 and Judg. 13:18).

The Bible talks a lot about knowing the Name—which is

to say, knowing God, knowing Him as He really is (Pss. 9:10; 91:14). God also knows men by name (Exod. 33:12). If we remember that "to know" always includes "to love," then we can understand that to know "the Name" really means to have a going relationship with God, to live one's life in covenant partnership with Him. To talk about the Name comes close to talking about the heart of the biblical message.

This is why the Name appears constantly in Israel's songs. To know the Name (*this* Name) inspires one to sing His praises (Pss. 69:30; 72:19; 74:21; etc.). God had said to Moses, "You will find out who I am." And Israel did find out what God's Name was. In the in's and out's of its history, it found out who and what God really was. Everything that was good, merciful, and faithful in His dealings with Israel got taken up in the word "Name." This is *the* word that characterizes God as the God of authentic, concrete, and experienced covenant partnership.

To know the *Name* involves making an appeal to the Name—making an appeal to God, the God whose great deeds are told and retold in Israel (I Sam. 12:22; Pss. 23:3; 25:11; 31:3; 79:9). Using a name this way signals the fact that a given name has become illustrious. "To thy name give glory" (Ps. 115:1). This means that His honor is at stake. The *Name* is the honor that Jahweh puts on the line in His decision to initiate His program of redemption.

Let's throw in another factor here. What does an expression like "making his name great" have to do with God's honor (II Sam. 7:26; Ps. 34:3)? Can mere man add anything or take anything away from the greatness of the *Name*? Surely not in the crude sense that men could decide whether or not God has a Name. But having a Name does suggest that God is willing to subject Himself, in a sense, to men's abuse. And what men can do with God's Name becomes terribly visible in their treatment of Jesus.

The Old Testament, too, gives us instances of how men can dishonor and secularize God's name (Exod. 20:7). But

God let people have His Name so they could give Him the honor that He always had and still has. He gives them His Name so that they can honor Him in *public*. God in His own being did not require man to "make his Name great." But He *chose* to need it. When Psalm 22:3 tells us that God is enthroned on the praises of Israel, it means just that. We have all learned to pray: "Hallowed be Thy Name." God depends on men to call on His Name and know Him as Holy.

All in all, the *Name is God*—God in His revelation, God in His coming to men. God in His revelation—this is a good way of putting it as long as we don't suggest that somewhere *behind* the revelation hides the *real* God, the essence, the very Godness of God. Not that! When Israel called on the Name, it meant that the real, the essential God was the God who came to men. In His introduction to us, He comes with His very essence. The Name is God.

To confess the Name of God means that one has experienced God. Let's not shrink that word "experience" down to a mere individualistic, inner-life, pietistic thing. God's revelation has taken place for us when we really know Him. And to experience it is to experience something that embraces our whole world.

29
Knowing

Another word we must learn to understand from the Bible itself is "knowing." What did the Bible writers mean by this word?

We should begin by noting what the Bible writers did *not* mean. They did not mean that a person got to "know" simply by studying a subject until he had mastered it. For the Bible writers a very important assumption lay behind knowing: to know someone or something entailed being personally involved with that person or thing. Without relationship there is no knowledge. To put it more strongly, to know someone is almost the same thing as to carry on a relationship with him. Thus the intimate sexual relationship between a man and a woman is called "knowing."

But this ground rule is present even in less intimate relationships. I Samuel 3:7 tells us that Samuel at that time had not yet come to "know" the Lord. Now Samuel had of course heard all sorts of things about Jahweh; he had learned just about everything that Eli could teach him. Not to know, then, meant not to have had a personal relationship—no matter how much one had learned with his head about Him.

Or let's take an example from the New Testament: "I do not know the man," says Peter in Mark 14:71. Peter did not mean to indicate that he had never heard of Jesus, did not know anything about Him. Everyone had gotten to know about this rabbi of Nazareth. What he wanted to insist on was this: I am not one of those men who travel around with Jesus; I don't belong to His group of friends.

We can use the word "know" in the sense of persons knowing each other. When we do, we mean to suggest that they carry on a relationship or friendship with each other. Teen-agers talk about "going with someone." And this hints at what the Bible means by knowing someone.

While we usually limit this personal sort of knowing to knowledge people have of one another, the Israelites talked this way about things and circumstances as well. I Samuel 16:16 says literally that David "knew" the harp. This did not mean that he knew how a harp was put together; it meant that he was a practiced player. Isaiah 53:3 says that the Servant of the Lord "knew" sickness; he knew from experience what it is like to be sick.

Knowledge (to take the noun) is not a theoretical mastery of some learned material. It is what Proverbs and Ecclesiastes mean when they talk of knowledge (Prov. 1:4, 22, 29; Eccles. 1:16-18; 2:21, 26). In both books knowledge and wisdom are mentioned together, and these rise from personal involvement.

To know God, then, means much more than to know that He exists. To know God means more than to be a qualified theologian. For the writers of the Bible it meant that one had a personal relationship with God—in love, trust, and obedience.

Let's take a few examples from the Old Testament. Here is a summons: "Know the Lord." This is really a call to engage in obedient, loving relationship with Him (a far cry from "Study theology"—as important as theology may be). This is why Isaiah's prophecy that Egypt and Assyria would one day know God was so rich and deep a prophecy (Isa. 19:19-25). Not only Israel, but even Israel's archenemies would be welcomed into God's friendship, enter God's covenant, and experience God's reality.

Jeremiah's word has the same stunning thrust. No one shall have to go about saying, "Know Jahweh!" Why not? "They shall all know me . . . says the Lord" (Jer. 31:34). When this happens, when this knowledge is found, God's covenant involvement with man will have been completed.

Turning to the New Testament, we find that John offers striking illustrations. In John 10, where Christ calls Himself the Good Shepherd, we read that the sheep know Him (vs. 4)—that is, live in trust of Him. And verse 14 says that He also knows the sheep. Following this comes the statement that Christ knows the Father and the Father knows Christ. This shows us that for John the word "know" points to a very intimate, personal relationship. We must read John 17:3 in this light: "And this is eternal life, that they know thee . . . ."

Clearly, knowing God is not the same as knowing some things about God with our intellects. One does not know

God when he has memorized a list of His attributes picked up from a book of theology. To know God is a practical experience. One knows God when he learns to appeal to God's attributes directly and personally. Our knowledge of God is directed towards our relationship with God, our romance with Him, and has to do with those dimensions of our experience that express our relationship; it has to do with love, with praise, with obedience, and with service. All of these together. We could say that our knowledge of God is one in which God keeps playing His own part as Covenant God and Lord, and is never reduced to the measure of a theological question.

"Israel does not know," says the Lord in Isaiah 1:3. Oh, they knew more about God than any other people knew. But they were disobedient in their relationship with Him; their knowledge did not include action, service, love, and obedient praise. Therefore it was really ignorance. Hosea 4:1 and 6:6 offer us the same picture: love and knowledge are all but the same thing.

The New Testament only adds more of the same. Look at I John 2:3-6, where knowledge of God equals service. And at I Corinthians 8:1-3, where knowledge without love is not real knowledge. In I Corinthians 13:2, Paul says the same thing. And in II Thessalonians 1:8, to be ignorant is to disobey. In I Timothy 1:3-7, Paul uses the phrase "sound teaching" (really, "healthy teaching") to indicate his desire that knowledge embrace obedience (see also Titus 1:16 and 2:1). Throughout, the New Testament carries on a vigorous campaign against a theoretical knowledge that tolerates the luxury of personal aloofness and spiritual disobedience.

The basic sense of the word "know" is underscored more heavily when the Bible writers talk about God's knowledge of us. Here are some typical examples: God knows Abraham (Gen. 18:19); God knows Israel (Amos 3:2); God knows the paths of the poet (Ps. 142:3). In all these, we see God in His trusting involvement with, His

loving relationships with, His caring for, those He knows.
Wonderful as it is to know God, it is much more wonderful
for God to know us (I Cor. 8:3). When God knows us, the
whole new reality of the life of promise begins.

30
The Glory of the Lord

Here is the climax. History ends with the revelation of
the "Glory of the Lord." But what does this mean?

Starting with ordinary language, "glory" points to someone's importance or excellence: a person's glory is what
makes him stand out in the crowd, what gives him standing, what brings him respect among his fellow men. We
often talk about "status symbols"—things that give one
standing. We can start with this.

What gives a man "status" among people? Lots of an-
swers can be given to this, most of them having to do with
something tangible. Jacob's glory lay in his property and
his goods (Gen. 31:1). Abraham, we are told, was "full of
glory" (so the Hebrew puts it) because of his cattle, gold,
and silver (Gen. 13:2). Psalm 49:17 sets glory and riches
next to each other as equals.

When the brothers told Jacob about Joseph's glory in
Egypt, they accented not his wealth, but his high post in
the land. "Glory" is also used this way in I Kings 3:13;
here riches and glory are separate things. The point?
Things other than property and wealth can give a man
status or glory.

There is talk of the glory of a people, too (Matt. 4:8). A
people's glory may consist in wealth (Isa. 60:11 and Rev.
21:24). But "glory" may refer as well to the position of

power that a people enjoys in the world (e.g., Moab in Isa. 16:14). What gives Israel a place of glory is Jahweh, Israel's God. Phinehas's wife understood this; notice the name she gave to her child when the ark of Jahweh was stolen: Ichabod, the glory has been taken away. That which gave Israel its glory, what made Israel Israel, was stolen (I Sam. 4:21, 22).

But glory is not only for men and nations. God too has His glory. Some Bible writers have a habit of talking about Jahweh's coming to the tabernacle or the temple in terms of the "appearance of his glory" (Exod. 40:34; Lev. 9:6; I Kings 8:11; Ezek. 1:28). They mean, of course, that Jahweh Himself appeared. They did not see Him appear materially; but they did see the thrust of His Godness. When it happened, it was so impressive that the writers spoke of it as the coming of a cloud that carried His glory. The temple is not great enough to contain His glory when it comes (I Kings 8:27). The whole earth is required for it, as the cherubs chant in Isaiah 6:3.

The glory of the Lord—this is a way of announcing Jahweh's tremendous "presence" in the midst of Israel. It can suggest His coming there to live. But His glory is revealed, too, in His actions; in what He *does* for Israel (Ps. 111:2). And what He does is great! Jahweh "glorifies himself" when He liberates Israel from Pharaoh's hands (Exod. 14:4 ff.). He "glorifies himself" in His judgment of the sinner who corrupts His handiwork (Lev. 10:3). Sometimes the writers say that Jahweh "sanctifies himself," shows Himself as the Holy One. What this means is that God creates respect for Himself (in the eyes of the peoples and their gods) by performing great deeds of judgment and liberation (see, e.g., Num. 20:2-13; Ezek. 20:41; 28:22).

The "glory of the Lord" usually calls up the picture of God in action, God as He is in His deeds. Whether it is God's action in nature or in human affairs does not matter for the Israelite; it is still the "Lord's glory." What we call nature was history for Israel—it was the history of God's faithfulness. "The Glory of God in Nature" (Beethoven) was not just the mirror of divine beauty; the Bible writers were not very romantic about nature. For them, nature witnessed to God's acts of faithfulness; its upkeep proclaimed the glory of God. This is how we should read Psalm 19:1. In Psalm 97:6 the Lord's glory is identical with His righteousness, and that is to say it is identical with what makes Him a true Covenant Partner.

From all this we can see why the Old Testament expectations for the future savor of glory. What do we wait for? What is the climax of history? The revelation of the "glory of the Lord" (Isa. 40:5), the whole earth full of His glory (Num. 14:21; Pss. 72:19; 57:5, 11; Isa. 66:18). The happy ending of history is the breakthrough of the great time of salvation, and *that* is the "glory of the Lord."

The New Testament couples its message with this when it proclaims that the time of salvation has broken in with the coming of Jesus Christ. In one sense, Isaiah 60:1 and 2 was fulfilled then and there. The glory of Jesus Christ is revealed because He is God in action, with decisive saving effects. The glory of Jesus Christ comes out not just in His resurrection, but in His cross—if one has eyes for this kind of glory. Together (see John 12:23 ff.), cross and resurrection reveal the glory of God (John 13:31, 32). Thus the history of Jesus makes it really clear, for the first time, that God glorifies Himself not at the expense of men, but for their good. His glory means our life, our salvation, our abundance.

Once we get this into our hearts, we will not stop glorifying God (Luke 2:20). Glorifying God—a final word about this. More literally, it is "giving God glory" (see Jer. 13:16; Pss. 29:1 ff.; 96:7 ff.; Rev. 4:11; 5:12). But God already *has* glory—this is His "status" among the gods and among men. To *give* God glory only means that we recognize and honor Him in the excellence He displays by His terrific acts of liberation, recognize and honor Him by means of the obedience and festivity His glory elicits from us. His glory, just as His name, needs people who are willing (and who dare) to lose themselves in it—people who believe that to live is to celebrate the glory of God! This is what it is all about. For us it is really exalting; we get our "status" at the point where we begin to see the glory of God (Ps. 3:4). The New Testament calls it the glorification of men; that is, our participation in the tangible excellence of God and His anointed (Col. 3:4; Rom. 8:17, 30). Then, and only then, will God be where He wants to be—and we with Him—His glory covering the whole earth. His glory—and ours!